VET FOR ALL SEASONS

Hugh Lasgarn grew up in a small Welsh village and trained at Glasgow Veterinary College. Since graduating, he has lived and worked in the Welsh Border country that he loves and where he met and married his wife. A devoted healer of animals great and small, he believes that the essential ingredient for a vet is not love of animals but respect for them, combined with the incentive to ease suffering and the courage to take life when pain is beyond control.

VET FOR ALL SEASONS

Hugh Lasgarn

FONTANA/Collins

First published by Souvenir Press Ltd 1986
First issued in Fontana Paperbacks 1987
Second impression May 1988

Copyright © 1986 by Souvenir Press Ltd

Printed and bound in Great Britain by
William Collins Sons & Co. Ltd, Glasgow

In the space of four seasons a man can rub shoulders with success and failure; hope and despair; pride and humility; life and death.

Such a man . . .

. . . is a country vet.
Hugh Lasgarn
February 1986

To Diana

1

If nothing else, on that summer Saturday I was the best dressed vet in the whole of the Welsh Borders. Indeed, it would have been a fair wager that, even further afield, my sartorial elegance would have been quite unique in the profession. For who else could be speeding to an urgent case of Milk Fever attired in top hat and tails, grey gloves and a pink carnation?

To be strictly accurate, the topper and gloves were lying on the rear seat, the little Ford not being lofty enough to accommodate such headgear, and the gloves I had not even worn, but the pinstripes, white shirt, grey tie and pearl-buttoned waistcoat were very much on show.

Such was the urgency of my visit, however, that on arrival at Holyoak Farm, I was out of the car and round to the boot before I realised I had halted in a sea of wet, smelly, agricultural mud—muck, to be more precise—the disgusting terrain was adhering like treacle to my patent-leather shoes. As it happened, the Moss Bros, hired trousers were not an ideal fit which, for once, was a blessing. By finishing their descent some three inches above my shoes, they avoided an encounter the like of which they had never experienced, or were ever likely to at any future function they attended.

'Come on, Ivor!' I shouted across the yard. 'Where's the cow? I'm half-way through a wedding!'

Ivor Barret poked his head round a doorway and blinked. Then, without a word, he appeared in full, took a few paces forward, halted and rubbed his balding pate with a calloused hand.

Stripping off the tails, I pulled on my wellington boots, grabbed my case, brown smock and bottle of calcium and turned to confront him.

'Come on, Ivor!' I repeated. 'I'm in a hurry and half-way through a wedding.'

The old boy nodded. 'Very good of you to come, Mr Lasgarn, I'm sure,' he said, his eyes seemingly transfixed by my pearl-buttoned waistcoat. 'She's in 'ere.'

I asked him to get a bucket of hot water to bring the calcium up to blood heat, then made for the shed.

The little brown cow lay uneasily on her side in the small square loose-box. Her stomach appeared ballooned with gas and I decided she was best sat up, for the presence of an inflated rumen in her semi-conscious state could cause severe embarrassment to both heart and lungs. Sitting the patient up and supporting her with straw bales would encourage belching and easing of the wind.

'Did'n really expect her to go down,' said Ivor, as he kneed a second bale tighter to her shoulder. 'Calved two days now, an' I thought she'd be past it. But then,' he rubbed his stubbly chin, briefly, ''er mother was the same, in fact, the whole family are like it!'

Fidget, for that was her name for obvious reasons, though her present condition was far from active, turned sleepily, as if to rebuke the aspersions cast upon her relatives. But the calcium deficiency from which she was suffering was rapidly taking its toll on her muscle strength and her head flopped heavily to one side.

'It's the Jersey in her,' I commented. 'That makes a big difference. They're always odd when it come to Milk Fever.'

Indeed, as a breed, that was true, probably because, in the main, they were like little grass-eating milking machines on legs. Not only was the milk of outstanding quality, but when it came to output, their productivity, weight for weight, could be quite phenomenal. Little

8

wonder that their bodies were often starved of the essential elements at calving time, calcium being the main one, with phosphorus and magnesium often low as well.

As these minerals were vital for the positive action of all muscles, including those of the heart and stomach as well as the ones attached to the skeleton, their depletion caused the patient to enter a state of collapse—like a puppet whose strings had become slack. As a result, the unfortunate beast was unable to stand, the stomach failed to force out excess gas, the heart became weak and the consequences were fatal, unless help was at hand—which explained the urgency of my mission.

Fortunately, the replacement of warm calcium solution into the jugular vein, aided by the rubber flutter-valve injection apparatus, was rapid in its effect. By the time the fluid had left the bottle, the sparkle was already returning to Fidget's eyes and she was sitting up and looking decidedly brighter.

One of the signs that the calcium was working right through the body was the production of small beads of moisture on the nose, for the sweat glands there, controlled by minute muscles, became paralysed due to the deficiency, leaving the muzzle abnormally dry. I knelt down in front of the little Jersey's face and peered closely, to check the response.

But Fidget indicated her recovery in a far more dramatic manner, by giving vent to a massive belch of foul stomach gas that took me completely by surprise, enveloping my whole person in an invisible cloud, as deadly in its concentration as it was repulsive in its odour.

I knew, instinctively, it would be my bosom pal for the rest of the day.

Telling Ivor not to milk his cow until the following morning to allow the calcium reserves to replenish, I washed the injection kit in the bucket, rinsed my hands, dried them on my smock and made for the car. I decided not to change back into my shoes until I was well clear of the yard.

Ivor, who had followed me, eyed the hat, gloves and crumpled tails lying on the rear seat, with interest. 'Please apologise to Mrs Lasgarn . . .' he put a hand to his mouth. ' 'Ad you got that far?' he asked, hesitantly.

'That far . . .?'

'Ay. Married,' he said.'

I couldn't suppress a smile as I explained that it was not *my* wedding, but a girlfriend of my fianceé, Diana. The reason I had been called out was that McBean, the senior assistant, had gone to Ireland, his father having died earlier in the week. Bob Hacker, the principal, had said he could manage, but as was often the case when short-handed, the day had turned out to be extremely busy. Consequently, when I came out of church, I found a note under the wiper of the little Ford, asking me to go to the 'Milk Fever'. Diana had gone on to the reception with friends and I intended to follow as soon as I could.

I wondered whether Ivor had thought I was dedicated or crazy.

'That's all right, then,' he said, as if spoiling any day off but my own wedding was of no consequence. Then his face wrinkled and he rubbed his chin thoughtfully.

'What's the matter?' I asked.

'Don' suppose you've got time to look at a lame cow?'

My sense of humour evaporated. 'No, I haven't,' I retorted.

'Well, p'raps it don' matter, now,' he continued casually. ' 'Er's been lame a fortnight—I'll see how she goes.'

I drove off down the lane, thinking what inconsiderate, thick-skinned old farts farmers could be at times.

Well clear of Holyoak, I found a dry patch of road just before the railway bridge and did a quick change, much to the amusement of some passing cyclists, one of whom went into a ditch as a direct result of his curiosity.

10

The spectacle did much to restore my lost sense of humour.

By the time I reach the Penalty Hotel, five miles the other side of Ledingford, I was entire but crumpled. I had done the best I could with the shoes, using my brown smock as a convenient duster. The rest of my garb was reasonably presentable, although my white collar was creased and a single spot of muck had found its way onto the centre of my light grey tie, despite having tucked it inside my shirt for safety. As I made for the hotel door, I reflected that it was the very place where some people wore diamond-studded pins; but then, I reasoned, country vets were different.

Up the broad-flighted steps I sprang and through the swing door to the foyer, which was empty. The guests, I concluded, were already seated.

I was about to investigate further when a red-faced, tail-coated figure appeared from a side room. It was Mr Blane, the bride's father, whom I had briefly met a few evenings previously when Diana and I had delivered our present.

'Sorry I'm late,' I apologised. 'Had a call.'

'You've missed the sherry, old boy,' he replied, jovially. Then he lifted up his right index finger and froze momentarily as if playing 'statues'.

'Got it!' he exclaimed suddenly, coming to life again. 'In there—help yourself.' Giving me a broad wink, he added, 'Just off to make a call. Wedding Bells in the two-thirty at Worcester—worth a try!'

'Put a pound on for me,' I called with a laugh, as he dashed away down an adjacent passage; then, following his instructions, I went into the side room where, to my instant delight, I discovered a lone waiter surrounded by a sea of glasses, dispensing champagne.

'Bride's father said I was to help myself,' I explained. He eyed me suspiciously, then shrugged his shoulders and continued pouring.

So help myself I did—fully. After all, I had missed the sherry.

I should have guessed that something was odd when the waiter suddenly ceased his labours and put down the bottle with a loud thud, making its contents fizz up merrily and overflow. Then, giving me what I could only describe as a nauseating look, with a great 'huff' he pushed open an adjacent window.

It was only when I joined the guests that the reason for his somewhat precipitous action became clear. For when Diana, who saw me enter, came across, she said: 'Oh, darling, I'm so glad you've made it.' Then she stood back a pace, swallowed gently, leaned forward and, kissing me on the cheek, murmured: 'Pooh! Don't you stink!'

Under normal circumstances I would have felt distinctly embarrassed, but with four glasses of Moët et Chandon under my belt I didn't mind one bit. I was merely conscious of some enquiring glances amongst the immediate company, which seemed to say, 'We know who it is and what it is—but can't quite make out where it is.' Fortunately Mr Blane's hospitality was as overwhelming to his other guests as it had been to me, and before long everyone was all smiles and chatter and my personal aroma of no further general concern.

Even if my condition had detracted in any way from the enjoyment of the occasion, it would have been admirably compensated by Mr Blane who, just after the bride and groom had departed for their honeymoon, came over and pushed a small bundle of notes into my hand—Wedding Bells had come in at twenties! For him, the valiant little filly paid for the whole grand affair, whilst for me, my unexpected good fortune adequately covered the hire of my suit, the present and a good night out afterwards.

In fact, our day ended in the small hours of Sunday morning and, as we kissed goodnight, Diana said sleepily, 'I love you, Hugh Lasgarn—even if you do stink. But just one thing . . . At our wedding, you don't work!'

And when we did get married twelve months later, I made damned sure I had the day off.

2

Diana and I had become engaged in the March of that year, just over twelve months after I had come to Ledingford. It was on the first day of spring and we had driven out to the Black Mountain which, for me, had now cast away the sinister symbolism of my first acquaintance, presenting a more agreeable, even comforting background to the rural environment.

At that stage I was in the springtime of my career as well—like the seed corn, sprouting upwards hesitantly but purposefully, still fresh and green but steadily maturing. Although my initial term in agricultural practice at Ledingford was originally to have been but thirty days, the demise of Bob Hacker's father, my temporary deferment, then the repeal of National Service had altered my prospects considerably. Indeed, my outlook had changed from uncertainty and insecurity to a more settled view and, like the seed corn, I was even beginning to put down roots.

There was no doubt that Diana was a major influence upon my pattern of living; although during the daytime I was very much wrapped up in my work, there was never a moment when some part of my thinking was not occupied with the 'blonde on the piano stool', a picture firmly etched upon my mind from the first time I had set eyes upon her.

Because time off was limited by normal standards, she often came along when I did evening or weekend calls, although, looking back, I sometimes wonder why she continued to do so, when I think of some of the veterinary experiences to which she was subjected in those early days.

14

Take the case at Wormcastle.

Wormcastle Farm, with Reg and Harry Bayne, represented a cornerstone in my career, for it was one of the first farms I visited when I came to Ledingford.

I well remember Bob Hacker looking down at the appointment book and saying:

'Now, where shall we send you today? Let's see . . . Wormcastle, Reg and Harry. Yes, Wormcastle . . . losing ewes, wasting and dying. Good farmers, but a bit old-fashioned. Yes, Hugh, you go to Wormcastle and try that one.'

I had set off, rehearsing the causes of wasting and death in ewes, as for a final examination. So thorough was my revision that, when I turned into the farm lane, I had thought of seventeen possible diagnoses.

Wormcastle was tucked away amid the northwest folds of Herefordshire, some two hundred gently undulating acres, bordered by the river on the south side, with the remnants of Offa's Dyke skirting the western border. The fields were varied in size and oddly shaped, divided by tight hawthorn hedges and dotted with small coppices and plantations that gave cover for a multitude of wildlife, pheasant and fox alike.

For the most part, the building still comprised its original plan as when first erected in the mid-sixteenth century; time, however, had not only weathered its countenance but also played merry tricks with the perspective.

Slit-eyed windows squinted at all angles, doorposts and pock-marked lintels crouched lopsidedly beneath the weight of sagging roofs. The aged, moss-covered tiles had mainly been replaced with slates just before the Second World War, but within, the stalls and mangers that had housed generations of Wormcastle cattle stood as always, solid and silent as chapel pews.

Although close to the Border, when the wicked Welsh

mist swirled about the yards it could find no way to penetrate the dark, pungent, animal-warm, secretive interior of the sheds. They were safe and secure . . . in Border terms, 'cwtchy'.

The farm was owned and run by the brothers, both bachelors in their mid-fifties. They had lived under the thumb and strap of their father to whom hard work was God's gift, a bounty to be received with open arms . . . and he made sure that Reg and Harry were never short of the Good Lord's benevolence.

But their father had died ten years past, two months after the Foot and Mouth outbreak. It never came to Wormcastle, but the fear of the scourge and all its terrible consequences were too much for the old man to bear, and he went to his Maker one April morning, with his sleeves rolled up and his braces tight, after collapsing in the duckpond.

Mother went three months after; a quiet, diligent, shrunken woman, who had the doubtful good fortune to be stone deaf and so avoided her husband's tongue as it rolled out sermons, orders, country philosophies and occasional oaths onto the bowed heads of Reg and Harry.

Since that time, the 'boys' had had a succession of house-keepers, who had come to Wormcastle for various reasons and with sundry ambitions of how to handle a situation that was as set in its pattern as the River Wye.

There was the retired schoolmistress from Salford, who treated them both like naughty children; said fat bacon was unhealthy and dogs should never be allowed in the kitchen. She left after they killed a pig in the back yard and their foxy dog bit her in her Sunday best.

Then there was the little, smiling blonde from Bristol, who brightened up the whole place and made their lives much happier. But, as Reg put it: ''Er picked up summat from one of the local lads, that made 'er sick every mornin'.' So she went back to Bristol. After several more unfortunate experiences, they finally gave up and settled for Daisy

Burns, the keeper's wife, who came and 'did' for them two days a week.

When I arrived on my first visit, I had found Harry, hands deep in the pockets of his patched, brown stock coat, leaning against the rough cowshed wall, right shoulder taking his weight, one leg bent at the knee, the other rigid, with both boots planted firmly on the mudcovered cobbles.

From a distance one could easily have thought by his posture that, if he had walked away, the building would have fallen to the ground.

After introducing myself, to which he showed little reaction, I commented upon the weather.

'There's only one thing certain about a day like today,' he mused. 'The mist'll clear an it'll rain afore twelve. Early mornin' mists always turns to rain afore twelve till the blackthorn's out.'

To Harry, that was an undisputed fact of country lore: the blackthorn was not out, the mist would clear and it would rain before twelve.

'You've been losing sheep,' I said, putting down my case.

He nodded.

'How many?' I asked.

'A few,' he replied, still not altering his posture.

'How many's a few?' I enquired.

Harry shrugged, still leaning against the wall. 'Couple or three,' he replied, and I realised that was as near as I would get.

In fact, the numbers game in Herefordshire was something I soon had to learn, otherwise the practice would have been well out of pocket.

For some peculiar reason, farmers were reluctant to give an accurate count. Maybe it was born of the uncertainty of life when dealing with livestock; for indeed, there was always a very obvious degree of caution exercised whenever any statement was made regarding their number or condition.

17

If one enquired about the health of the stock, they were mostly non-committal, prefacing their reply with: 'Well, the last time I saw them . . .' even if it was only an hour ago, for some catastrophe might well have struck since, '. . . they were middlin' to fair.' I remember once asking a client how his bull was and he said:

'Well, it's difficult to rightly say, for every time I looks at 'im, 'e's either standin' up or lyin' down.'

Anyway, after some months in the country, I learned that 'a few' was up to three; 'a fair few' was up to seven; 'quite a few' could be fifteen to twenty, and a 'good few' from twenty upwards.

The other accounting problem occurred when groups of animals had been treated and the total tally had to be taken, for pricing the job.

To ask was useless, for they were never sure and might get off lightly if they left the count to the vet, who was often too busy to be absolutely accurate. But I used to exaggerate knowingly saying fifty when I knew it was well under forty, and they soon came up with the correct number.

If you did get 'done', it was rarely through dishonesty, for it was all part of the game that made country dealing and wheeling so interesting.

When collecting cash, there was no discount, but 'luck money', and if you hadn't added that factor in beforehand—you were the unlucky one!

I was about to ask to see the sheep when Reg emerged from the house, accompanied by a foxy looking dog who immediately circled me suspiciously, then lay down a few yards away, ready to herd me into any direction his master dictated.

'Mr Lasgarn, the new vet,' announced Harry.

'Misty old morning,' I said, stepping forward to shake Reg's hand.

'It'll not clear till dusk,' said Reg, confidently. 'Never does this time o' year when the moon's fillin.' Another fact

18

of country lore, which somewhat contradicted Harry's version, but apart from shifting his weight to the other leg, Harry made no comment.

Not that Harry was dumb, not by a long way; when he worked a dog to round up cattle, he could shout and holler as good as any in the county. And, as I later found out, talking to him on his own, he could discuss current affairs and 'polotics', and chat about Anthony Eden, Ike and 'Ole Khruschev', as if they lived just up the road.

But when Reg was around Harry, who was two years his junior, usually shut up.

For it was Reg who made all the decisions, ordered the goods, drove the car and cracked jokes, and it was Harry who mostly just nodded his head, carried the sacks, sat low in the passenger seat and squeezed out silent smiles at his brother's rustic humour.

I can't for the life of me remember whether the mist did clear before twelve or last until dusk, so I never knew who was right, for I was soon involved in a *post mortem* examination of the dead sheep that lay covered with sacks in the wagon shed.

They watched closely and silently as I dismembered the carcase, assessing my capability with the knife and my familiarity with the unfortunate animal's internal organs. But I hadn't far to look, for the liver was rock hard and fibrosed, and when I cut into the pipe-stem bile duct, a score of thumbnail-sized, flat, fleshy liver fluke streamed out.

Satisfied that this was the cause of death and relieved that it was something obvious and readily explainable, I told them all about it.

I told them how part of the fluke's life cycle was spent as a small cyst in the body of one particular freshwater snail, *Lymnéa truncatula,* to be precise. But I omitted to mention the Latin name in case I distanced myself by seeming to appear too academic.

But I did explain how the small snail, being freshwater, inhabited streams and boggy fields, of which Wormcastle had several, and how, when the cystic form left the snail, it climbed onto blades of grass and was usually eaten by the sheep.

If its luck was in and this happened, it then burrowed through the intestinal wall to reach the liver, where it matured and lazed away the rest of its fluky days, laying eggs to its heart's content and damaging its unsuspecting host irreparably.

I can see their faces now, when I announced that, in my opinion, sheep could never be farmed successfully at Wormcastle, unless they embarked upon an efficient fluke eradication programme.

Concluding my edict, I waited for comment. There came none. Even the foxy dog lay perfectly still.

'Fools rush in,' I thought, 'I've blown it.' I had been too outspoken. Fancy a young vet, green as grass, telling two seasoned sheepmen that they couldn't do something that they'd been doing for years. I realised I had a lot to learn regarding countryside diplomacy.

Reg pushed his cap backwards across his head and scratched his ear, and the foxy dog stood up and whimpered with impatience, but it was Harry who broke the silence. He dug his hand into his smock coat pocket and pulled out a small assortment of articles; there was a bit of pencil, a hazelnut, a staple, what looked like a calf scour pill and a piece of string. He studied the mix for a moment, then put it all back in his pocket, sighed and said:

'Well, I bin farmin' ship since I was knee high to a cow pat an' I never knew that.'

I sent some samples to the laboratory to ensure that I hadn't missed anything, but fluke was proved positive and the flock were duly drenched with a curative, to which they responded well.

From then on, I could do no wrong at Wormcastle.

I looked forward to every visit I made to the Bayne brothers. Although, to the casual observer, they took a bit of 'knowing', and such virtues as fortitude, resilience, honesty, and even a degree of serenity, were not immediately recognisable, nevertheless, as a good stockman 'knew' animals, it was a good lifeman who 'knew' people, and once you 'knew' Reg and Harry you realised their true worth.

Noncommittal they certainly were, in common with most of their countrymen.

'Where will you be?' I would often ask, when a request for a visit was made.

'If it's dry, us'll be plantin'.'

'If it's foine, us'll be harvestin'.'

'If it's snowin', us'll be feedin'.'

'If it's wet, us'll be spud sortin' . . . us don' rightly know where us'll be . . . depends on the weather.'

They watched for red skies, blackthorns, moons waxing and waning, cows lying down, cows standing up, berries on bushes and crows flying westward.

They knew the signs, although didn't always agree as to their significance. 'If yer can see that old Black Mountain clear, it be goin' to rain . . . an' if yer can't see 'im—' then they'd grin and rub their horny hands, vigorously, '— well, it be rainin' . . . in it?'

They had no family crest, but the basis of their philosophy, which had held good for generations, was encapsulated in the message embroidered on a framed tapestry that hung in the Wormcastle kitchen:

> Frozen ground man cannot dig,
> Snow that blinds, he cannot see,
> Rains that lash, his spade to rust,
> Sun to parch his land to dust,
> Wind to blow the crop away,
> Dawn to bring another day.

But, despite that rather depressing set of maxims, they were possessed of a cautious optimism and a respect for nature.

'Yer got to be self supportin',' Reg would say. 'Put back what yer takes. Mustn't force nature, you see. Lead 'er, but not force 'er. Just like they nice young fillies I expect you gets yer 'ands on, Hugh! Just like they—eh, 'Arry?'

And Harry would widen his face by a good two inches either side, raise his rosy cheeks like little cider apples, so that his eyes disappeared behind the bushy slits that were his eyelids, part his lips to show an assortment of nutbrown teeth and raise his shoulders without making a sound.

The perfect mime for a chortle, cackle or laugh, but never a sound.

It was several months before I took my first 'young filly' there—and that was Diana.

And it was all because of Plum Five.

3

Plum Five was one of a long line of pedigree Herefords at Wormcastle, the herd having been founded by Great Grandfather Bayne nearly a century before. She was a fifth generation Plum, as her ear tattoo showed.

Plum Five had been showing signs of uneasiness for some time, and Harry had watched her since morning, as she stood alone in Rushy Meadow. She hung away from the other cattle, gazing beyond the river, the tight hedgerows and soft wooded hills, as if searching for an explanation of the urgent pressures and sharp blades of fleeting agony that raked her abdomen.

Harry knew heifers often found calf-birth more difficult than older cattle. The easy living on the rich water meadows, the gentle pattern of life, the placidity and contentment of the Hereford breed, all combined to make them rather overfat and none too well prepared for starting a family.

About midday, he had parted her from the rest of the herd, bringing her slowly across the pastures and up the rutted lane to the buildings. She had come sensibly and quietly, as if thankful for the opportunity to take her mind off the physical unrest that had come over her.

But the old, weathered countryman appreciated how she felt, for, born and bred at Wormcastle, Harry had attended countless births among the Herefords. He was of the 'old school'; his stockmanship had never come from books. It was a natural combination of dedication, instinct and experience.

My learning was of hormones that influenced the pituitary gland, that mysterious primaeval organ of the brain, which triggered a complex chain of bodily responses, resulting in birth. But to Harry, cows 'bagged up', 'went off in the bones' and 'dropped', a series of features that also resulted in a live calf.

However one looked at it, scientifically or naturally, it was a miracle, and ever since God created the beasts of the field, the fantastic process had been the same.

Within the little heifer, the neck of the womb was already relaxing and the thick elastic plug, that had faithfully guarded the entrance since conception, was dissolving away.

Smooth, deep contractions next developed, gradually increasing in frequency and intensity, so that the waters began to ripple with the gentle urgency of a lake before a storm.

Cautiously responding to the gradual change, the clenched form, low in the maternal depths, began to straighten its curved spine. Soft, untested muscles extended limbs, easing them out of the confinement they had suffered since first they were moulded.

As the contractions became more positive, the unborn was forced forward, feet first, head between knees.

There was, however, to be much ado before this new arrival 'hit the deck' at Wormcastle Farm. The way Plum Five was straining and groaning, her tail and back arched in a vital effort to force her offspring into the world, told Harry the birth was going to be difficult.

The 'waters' had broken just after five o'clock and by six he knew the calf should have been born, or at least showing a leg or even two . . . but there was nothing. For some considerable time Plum Five laboured, bearing down with her flanks, contracting her abdominal muscles. She had lain in the straw, put her front feet in the manger and pushed her head between her knees—all to no avail.

Finally she could do no more; she was exhausted and stood, head down and panting, her sweating hindquarters shivering after the constant exertion.

The light was fading in the low-beamed loose-box as Harry Bayne forked over the straw, filling the well that Plum Five had created in the middle of the floor. Leaning on the long handle, he studied the distraught heifer. Harry hated making decisions, but she couldn't go on like this—something had to be done.

'It's no good,' he muttered and, giving the straw a final flick, went into the yard and across to the house.

☆　　☆　　☆

When the call came, I had just commenced my study of the *Ledingford Times*, which I was finding more interesting week by week, as I became familiar with local people and places. It was a newsy type of paper, even bordering on the gossipy, everything from sales, obituaries and sports, to country comment and the usual smattering of court cases— generally concerning visitors who had succumbed to the effects of the local cider, the usual line of defence, being: 'I never drunk the stuff before, Your Worship, an' I didn't know it could catch hold like it did.'

Diana had come over to the digs for the evening and was busy being instructed by Brad, my landlady, in the intricacies of knitting a Fair Isle patterned pullover which, although I hadn't enquired, I assumed was for me.

'Calving at Wormcastle,' I announced, when I returned from the hall. 'Like to come?'

'Is it going to be very messy?' she enquired, still concentrating on her needles and not looking up.

'Might be,' I said. 'Difficult to say. It's a heifer, so it could be a bit of a pull.'

'Oh, the poor thing,' she said, putting down her knitting. 'Well, so long as I can stay in the car. I don't think I could

25

stand seeing it, if it's not going to be normal.'

'You'll have to get used to it, if you're going to be a vet's wife,' observed Brad, looking over the tops of her glasses. 'No good you having a weak stomach.'

'Well, dogs and cats and even sheep, I don't mind,' admitted Diana. 'But anything bigger I'll leave to Hugh . . . And if that won't suit you, Mr Lasgarn,' she said, standing up and brushing down her woollen skirt, poking her tongue out at me as she did so, 'you'll have to look for someone else!' She grinned.

'It suits,' I said. 'Come on . . . and bring your knitting.'

Forty minutes later, having left Diana in the little Ford, I was stripping off my shirt to examine Plum Five in a loose-box at Wormcastle. Harry had anticipated my needs, and the ever-necessary bucket of hot water, soap and towel were standing waiting. Following a slight intake of breath as I slipped on my cold rubber apron, a reaction I still could not suppress, I was ready to investigate the little heifer's condition.

My examination of the flaccid birth canal took several minutes. Then, gently, I withdrew my arm and straightened my back.

'Problems,' I said to Harry. 'We have problems.'

'That's why you'm here,' said Harry, trying to make a joke, for I was sure he didn't intend to be rude.

'The head's too big,' I observed, ignoring his banter. 'It won't come through the pelvis.'

I studied Plum Five for some time. At one point, she turned as far as the halter would allow and looked at me earnestly, as if awaiting my comments.

Harry stood motionless beside me.

One by one, I analysed the possible solutions. If the calf had been dead I could have dismembered it, but it was alive, for I had felt its head pluck back when I tweaked its nose.

It had to be a solution that would cause as little distress as possible to the mother and yet provide maximum chance for the calf to survive. I cast my vote, made my choice and undid the strap of my red, rubber apron.

'There's only one way,' I said quietly, still looking at Plum Five.

Harry cleared his throat. 'Caesarian?' he asked nervously.

'I'm afraid so,' I answered.

The old stockman gave a low whistle and looked down at the straw-covered floor.

Not that it would be the first caesarian at Wormcastle Farm. Twelve months previously, on Grand National Day, when gallant little Oxo, with Michael Scudamore, a local farmer's son, aboard, romped home winner and the county went wild with excitement, Harry and Reg had assisted Bob Hacker to deliver a heifer calf by caesarian, due to an irreversible twist in the mother's womb.

To Harry it had been a minor miracle.

But whilst he respected Bob Hacker as a surgeon and was mightily pleased with the result, he had not enjoyed the performance and did not relish attending another.

He was not squeamish by any means and had seen many a gory sight in his life, but he had felt slightly giddy during the operation. Especially when Bob Hacker was cheerfully explaining the origin of the technique, as he worked busily away: how it was reputed that Julius Caesar had been born by direct surgical intervention into his mother's womb; and how, according to Bob, it was a Swiss pig castrator who carried out the first officially recorded operation—not, as one might have expected, upon a pregnant sow, but upon his own wife.

Perhaps it had been the conversation, or perhaps the smell of the anaesthetic in the confined space—he had managed to stick it out, but remembered how thankful he had been to get out into the yard and gulp lungfuls of fresh, clean air.

27

So, unbeknown to me, it was with a deep breath, a brave face and a knot in his stomach that he said, 'Well, Hugh, what'll you need?'

I stood back and surveyed my rustic operating theatre.

Above me, the aged beams, bowed from years of bearing the regular pressures of the granary aloft, their dark shadows hiding the cobwebbed ceiling boards, save where the feeble rays of a single, dust-covered electric bulk weakly penetrated.

My eye ran down the stone wall to the wooden manger and the big iron ring, to which Plum Five's halter was tied, then onto the cobbled floor, amply covered with crisp, yellow straw.

'The same scene for centuries,' I thought, 'and unlikely to change now.'

I could see old bushy-eyebrowed Professor Jennings, Head of Surgery at Glasgow, thumbs hooked in his waist-coat pocket, gazing over the heads of the Final Year students and proclaiming to the heavens:

'In "real" veterinary practice there are no ambulances to rush complications to modern, sterile operating theatres—cases must be dealt with, where and whence they come. Apart from a sound scientific and logical approach to his work, a country veterinarian's greatest assets will lie in his own initiative, common sense and courage.' Then the dear old mentor would return to earth, peer over his spectacles, inhale mightily and boom: 'Veterinary Science, gentlemen, is a discipline—remember that! Remember, when you are called upon to work amid conditions you would normally abhor. Remember at these times to adhere to your integrity, do your best and be not afraid.'

He always gave an oration worthy of a great roar of applause, which he duly got; he would then smile benevolently and raise his hand like some great political champion, until silence reigned again.

I broke my reverie and scanned the 'sterile' premises. Trying to clean it up would create more air pollution than already existed . . . it was best left.

'Be not afraid,' I reminded myself, 'and thank God for antibiotics!'

Harry, who was still at my side, repeated his previous question more confidently.

'We'll need extra light,' I said, 'and help.'

'There ain't nobody.' Harry screwed up his cheeks. 'Reg is skittlin' at the 'Shoes . . . League Finals . . . won't get 'im back. Place could burn down on Skittles Nights afore he'd leave 'is game.'

'Makes it difficult,' I said. 'Someone will have to stand at her head, and I could do with another pair of hands here.'

'I'll try 'im, if you like,' said Harry. 'I could phone. 'E'll be back in ten minutes if 'e'll come, an' I'll get a couple of Tillys from the house at the same time.'

He disappeared through the door.

I watched poor plum as she hung her head wearily, shuffling her limbs in an attempt to find a more comfortable position.

Then I went back to the car.

'I'm going to operate,' I told Diana. 'The calf is too big, it's going to have to come out through the side.'

'Oh!' she gasped. 'How awful!'

'It's the only way,' I said a little abruptly, the tension of the situation just beginning to grip me. 'I shall be at least an hour. I expect you can sit in the house, if you like.'

'I'm all right here,' she replied. 'The roof light is enough, so long as your battery will stand it.'

'Should do,' I said, sharply. 'You'll have to push me if it doesn't.'

And with that, I went round to the boot, collected all the kit and took it back to the loose-box. It had, just, crossed my mind to ask Di to help, but it wasn't really fair; although I hoped the operation would be surgically efficient, to the uninitiated it was bound to be 'messy', and no mistake. If Reg wouldn't come, then I'd manage by myself. Certainly, of the three others I had done, Bob had helped me with two and McBean with the other. But I didn't fancy calling them out to help, for I knew they always managed alone and I thought it was about time I did as well.

I had acquired a stainless steel box in which to keep my instruments, and that included a clean linen sheet which I spread over two straw bales to form a rustic instrument trolley. Out of my case I took disinfectant and pessaries and, from the calving box, some ropes. Flicking open the clasp of the stainless steel box, I checked my tools: scalpel; eight artery forceps to arrest haemorrhage in cut vessels; rack-toothed forceps to hold fine tissues; needle holders; scissors; catgut for uterine sutures; nylon for muscle and skin; needles and swabs.

Finally, I checked that the white-capped bottle of Xylocaine was full and I wondered how they managed before local anaesthetic—difficult to get a cow drunk or to bite on a bullet.

Taking a few millilitres of local anaesthetic, I swabbed the area just in front of Plum Five's tailhead in preparation for the epidural.

'Right, my dear,' I said. 'Just a little shot to relax you during the performance. Can't have you straining too much during the critical moments, can we?'

She barely moved as I inserted the fine needle towards the spinal nerve, for after her vain effort to calve, she was simply too fatigued.

I put the bottle back in the box and checked the equipment once more.

'Come on, Harry,' I said to myself, rubbing my hands impatiently together. 'Where are you?'

I took my watch from my pocket: five minutes to nine.

Waiting to get started was always a frustration; the

30

adrenalin was up, instruments ready . . . and no help.

But then, it was useless getting steamed up about it. If there was one thing I had learnt about country life in the Welsh Borders, it was, not exactly *mañana, mañana*, but not far from it. Professor Jennings should have added patience to his list of veterinary assets . . . there certainly was a lot more to being a country vet than people often thought. Folk would say: 'I should have been a vet, I love animals,' as if that was the sole requirement.

'It isn't love you want at the moment, is it, girl? It's action. You've had too much of the other stuff already!'

As I stroked Plum's trembling back, I was aware of the door creaking ajar and was about to round on Harry to regale him for the time he had taken, when a voice said:

'Do you want any help?'

It was Diana. She came forward out of the shadows and as she did so, a pale shaft of light from the struggling bulb caught her face.

She really was an attractive girl. Just nineteen, blue eyes, high cheek bones, which I had always admired so much in continental women, and blonde hair falling about her shoulders; she could easily have been Swiss or Scandinavian.

But before I could say anything there was a shuffling from outside and the bright light of a Tilly lamp carved a sharp, white beam through the gloom.

'Can' get no bloody reply from the 'Shoes,' said Harry. 'They must be all pissed out of their . . .' His eyes fell upon Diana. 'Oh!' he said, dropping both hands and the Tillys to his sides, so that, in the comparative darkness, only our feet were illuminated. 'Oh!' he repeated. 'Oh! My word!'

'This is Diana,' I said, taking one Tilly from him and holding it up. 'She'll give us a hand.' Then I turned back to her. 'You are sure?' I asked again. 'I mean, after what you said . . . but I certainly could do with some help.'

She nodded, her lips tightening as a nervous smile

crossed her face. As I watched her reaction, I felt myself gripping my hands together and squeezing the palms, unconsciously testing the strength of my fingers for the task ahead.

'You know what I'm going to do?' I asked again, still doubting that her presence was wise. I was in no way a chauvinist and admired her guts for coming, but she looked so vulnerable and feminine that I felt it was wrong to involve her in such an affair.

'A caesarian,' she said.

'Do you mind the sight of blood?'

I suddenly realised how little I knew about Diana, at least about her emotions and inner feelings. Young love soars upon a magic carpet of delightful trivia, not actually contemplating the harsh realities of life. How many suitors, I wondered, had ever posed that question in the early days of courtship? Not many, I concluded.

'Will there be much?' she asked, her lips tightening further, as a barely perceptible quiver ran through her body.

'Not a lot,' I replied, as reassuringly as I was able. 'But we'll have to get you some different togs if you're going to be a "real" assistant.'

Harry, who was still looking somewhat confused, but obviously relieved that he would now be able to stay at the head and away from the action, hung his Tilly on a hook on a beam. Then, wiping his horny hands in his smock, he touched his cap and said, 'Pleased ter meet you, miss,' and held out his hand.

'Pleased to meet you, too,' replied Diana, sweetly.

They shook hands. The very politeness of the introduction was slightly incongruous in view of the impending drama.

'I can get a coat for you and there's a pair of Daisy's boots, what she leaves when she comes up—just fit you, miss. Won't be long.'

As he made for the door, he half-turned and looked directly at me.

'My word!' he said. 'My word!'

Then, he was gone.

Diana walked up to Plum and stroked her gently on the flank: 'You poor old thing,' she said sympathetically. 'Never mind, Hugh will do his best for you.' Then she faced me again. 'It is the only way, is it?' she added, as if she was having second thoughts.

'Well, at the moment, the calf is alive,' I explained. 'I felt it move when I examined her. But with the head resting on its knees, the whole body mass is too large for her pelvic bones. I could attach pulleys to the legs and try forcing it, but I know from experience that it isn't always successful. If it comes easily, then everything is all right, but if not, we could finish up with a dead calf and a paralysed mother. That's why I think caesarian is the most sensible and humane course.'

'How . . . how do you do it?' she asked hesitantly.

'The position of the incision depends upon the situation of the calf,' I continued. 'I can use either right or left side, but in this case, the calf's hind feet are turned towards the lower right flank and that's where I'll go in. Plum is tired but reasonably fit, so I shall operate with her standing, under local anaesthetic.'

My last statement obviously disturbed her, for she gave a slight gasp, and murmured, 'Standing.'

'Yes. When I enter the abdomen, the pressure inside can force the coils of intestine out through the incision, like an avalanche, especially if Plum should start to strain. I've already given her an injection that I hope will control that, but if it does occur, it's easier to deal with in the vertical position.'

I watched Diana's reaction closely. She moistened her upper lip with the tip of her tongue:

'Why don't you use a general anaesthetic?'

33

'Well, firstly, because she'd go down and I'd have problems with the intestine, and secondly, because general anaesthesia can be dangerous in cattle.'

I explained to her that, in a prostrate anaesthetised ruminant, the stomach could fill with gas, similar to a milk fever, and a swollen rumen could press upon the chest and cause heart failure. If there had been more time, I could have had her starved or even used an endotracheal tube. Diana frowned. 'That's a tube down the wind-pipe,' I told her, 'to stop her being sick . . . but it's still a bit dodgy. With local she'll hardly feel a thing after the first needle, and when I've finished, she won't have so much of a hangover.' A faint smile brushed Diana's face. 'Now, I would like you to hand me the instruments and swabs as I need them. There aren't many.

'Any questions?' I asked, and realised that I had spoken rather sharply. I should have to control my own nerves if I expected her to retain her composure. I took both her hands in mine. 'Do you think you'll be all right?' I asked, but this time more gently.

I had to give her every chance to back out if she wished. She might faint or be sick, which would leave me without an assistant. But far more important to me than that was that it might upset her . . . and that was the last thing I wanted.

Diana nodded and squeezed my hands, as another minute quiver crossed her shoulders; but there was determination in her blue eyes and I knew that she would be all right.

There was a kick, and the door banged open. Harry entered, carrying a steaming bucket of water in one hand, a pair of black wellies in the other and a brown smock over his arm.

'Ain't very posh,' he said, grinning, 'but it'll keep the shi . . . dirt off'n you. An' there's plenty of water if you need it.'

He put down the bucket and boots, then held the smock

up in front of him, as if showing it off in the manner of a high-fashion couturier—the action must have been quite spontaneous, for the nearest Harry Bayne had ever been to ladies' garments would have been a jumble sale at the church.

'Shears to clip the hair,' I interrupted.

'In the sheephouse, I'll get 'em,' he said. Handing Diana the smock, he disappeared again.

Ten minutes later, Harry had expertly clipped the operating area, while Plum Five stood resignedly, haltered to the manger.

Diana had tied her shoulder-length hair with the piece of string from Harry's pocket, probably the same piece I had chanced to see on my first visit, and, attired in the baggy brown smock, fronted with a spare red rubber apron I had in the car, she scrubbed the site diligently and swabbed it with spirit.

'Fine,' I said, filling the large syringe with anaesthetic. 'I'm going to deaden the nerves that run from the spine to the area of incision. It's called paravertebral anaesthesia. They run below these three vertebrae and I have to inject down onto them, separately.' I paused and tensed. 'Ready, Harry?'

Harry took hold of the halter and placed a gnarled hand upon Plum Five's wet muzzle.

'Easy, little lady,' he comforted. 'Us'll soon 'ave it from there.'

Ten minutes and the site was frozen. I stood poised, scalpel in hand like a conductor's baton, a starter's gun, a magician's wand—for at a drop of the wrist, the overture, the race, or even Harry's minor miracle, would commence.

This time, I didn't ask if they were ready, I just looked.

Harry nodded and turned his face to Plum Five's head. Diana took a deep breath and murmured, 'Yes.' My hand dropped and the blade swiftly split the skin.

35

A straight, narrow, blood-filled streak suddenly sprung apart to reveal layers of glistening connective tissue, criss-cross patterns of arteries, veins and thick, rich-red masses of muscle.

The first incision was over.

For me, this was the most emotive part of any surgery — an act of committal, a point of no return and a supreme test of the depth of anaesthesia. Plum Five had tensed slightly, but showed no other reaction; some of the exposed muscles twitched involuntarily, but the infiltration had worked well — there would be no pain.

Perhaps it was this discovery that relieved Diana, for without being told she took a swab and mopped the open wound.

'Artery forceps ready. I'm going through and we'll probably hit a few "spurters" on the way.'

As I spoke, I made a further, deeper incision into the flank muscle and hit the first 'spurter'. A fine spray of blood flashed through the air. It deposited a bright red, moving line of dots down Diana's left temple, streaked across her cheek and, missing her neck, ran down the centre of her apron to the floor.

She froze. Her eyes glazed and she rocked a little.

'Artery forceps!' I shouted — and I did shout. Loudly. In fact, I shouted three times before she appeared to hear.

'ANOTHER!' I bellowed.

She produced it.

'AND ANOTHER!' She became steadier and handed me the third one more positively. I turned to look at her, but she said nothing.

Seconds later and after a few more 'spurters', a puff of vapour signalled that I had achieved entry into the abdominal cavity; I enlarged the incision and stood back to admire my handiwork.

Through the artificial orifice, the internal workings of Plum Five's digestive system could be seen. To the right was situated the large rounded end of the great rumenal sac and below, centre, lay the churning sea of small bowel, with part of a kidney just visible above. But lying deep and to the left was the taut, irregular mass that was the foetal residence.

'There it is!' I exclaimed. 'A womb with a view!'

I thought it was quite a funny remark—but nobody laughed.

After washing up, I gently explored the interior.

The calf was alive all right; indeed, its vigorous wriggling within the protective bag made it difficult for me to bring any part of its anatomy up to the incision.

'Awkward little devil!' I announced. 'It's like a tadpole in here. If only it would keep still, things would be a lot simpler.'

Diana had taken on a new lease of life and even gave a quiet, nervous laugh as she peered over my shoulder into the living cavern.

Harry, however, was still at Plum's head, whistling softly, his back firmly to the whole proceedings.

I spent several strenuous minutes attempting to get the gravid uterus into position, but the calf wasn't having any. The activity was definitely contrary to its natural instincts. It wanted to go forward, not backward, and was determined to fight all the way.

'It's no good,' I gasped after one final, mighty exertion with both arms inside Plum's abdomen. 'I'll have to lift it up as far as I can and you'll have to cut into it. Grab that scalpel!'

Diana froze again. This time for but a fleeting second, but I sensed her reaction.

I threaded both arms back through the entry and cradled the heavy load. Then, with a mighty heave, I drew it upwards to the light.

'See where the feet are poking up?' I gasped. 'Cut along there!'

Diana passed the scalpel between my arms and into the

space, holding it over the exposed uterus.

'Cut!' I panted.

'I can't!' she sobbed.

'CUT!' I wailed, knowing I could not hold the heaving womb much longer.

'For God sake, cut, woman!' shouted Harry, still with his back turned.

Diana held her breath . . . and cut.

In a flash, a small right hind leg popped out. It was enough. I grabbed it, brought it to the outside and secured it with a rope.

Then it was all action. I took the scalpel from Diana's trembling hand, enlarged the incision, delved and retrieved the other hind leg which I roped as well.

'Harry!' I shouted. 'I need you!'

Together, we heaved the slippery body upwards and outwards through the gap in Plum's side and laid a fine, coughing and spluttering calf in the straw.

'Back legs!' I shouted, and Harry and I lifted and jerked the little creature up and down to clear its airways.

The two females gazed at the new arrival. The mother, eyes half-closed, with the incision still gaping in her side, and Diana, blood-spattered but smiling.

'Boy or girl?' she cried happily.

'It's a boy!' exclaimed Harry. Then, rather embarrassed at his own excitement, corrected it to: 'It's a bull calf . . . a fine bull calf.'

As soon as I was satisfied the calf was under its own steam, I turned my attention back to Plum Five.

'Now to close the gaps,' I said, as lightly as I could, 'and we're finished.'

After the delivery, the uterus contracted rapidly to about one tenth its previous size and I had to work speedily to sew and oversew my incision. By now Diana had lost all her inhibitions and held the cut edges together for me to insert the continuous line of catgut. She swabbed, trimmed, threaded needles and even inserted a pessary into the peritoneal cavity, under my supervision.

Harry, meanwhile, had been rubbing the calf with wisps of straw to dry his sticky red coat and stimulate the circulation; he stopped to watch the final suture being tied. Securing the knot, I held the uneven ends together between my fingers as Diana stood by with the scissors.

'Cut,' I said.

'Cut,' she replied, snipping the white strands with a smile.

I studied my impromptu assistant, arraigned in her gory ensemble as she shook her head, freeing a strand of hair trapped in the strap of her surgical apron. Still very feminine despite the surroundings, I thought, and gave her a wink.

Harry, whistling softly, pretended to be looking at Plum Five; Plum Five looked fondly at her son . . . and the little calf, for the very first time in his life . . . just looked.

After the drama came the tidying up. Not only the instruments and smocks, but the little bull, too, underwent his first wash and brush-up. A thorough one it was, as well, for Plum Five, now released, vigorously licked and nudged her new-born with joyous relief.

'That's the best tonic for 'er,' observed Harry. 'Nothin' like a live calf to put things right.'

'That goes for me, too,' I added, closing the lid of my instrument box.

'Yer can wash proper in the 'ouse,' offered Harry. 'Come on. I'll leave the light with 'em for now, an' straw 'em down later.'

As he led the way through the door, I turned to look at Diana as she gazed at the happy scene.

'She will be all right, won't she?' she asked, thoughtfully.

'Thanks to us, she's got a better chance than she had two hours ago,' I said. 'And I couldn't have managed it without you.'

She blushed. 'Of course you could.'

'Don't argue with the vet,' I chided and, taking her hand,
led her across to the house.

In the long, low kitchen, after several bowls of soothingly
soft hot water that lathered at the merest sight of soap, and
a rough rubbing with coarse linen towels, we both felt
cleaner and fresher. Following with steaming Camp coffee,
laced with Haig, we all relaxed around the fire.

Wormcastle kitchen was rather austere, the furniture old
and all the equipment and utensils well used; every piece
stood or hung alone—nothing blended.

The only redeeming features were the window and the
fireplace. In the west wall, a large picture window had
replaced the old heavy frame, looking out by day to a magnificent view across the Wye to the distant Black Mountain.

At the opposite end was an assortment of seating that
ranged from a large, sagging sofa and two cavernous armchairs, to a wooden stool and a plastic, folding seat. All
clustered around the open, stone fireplace that was cheerfully devouring large chunks of wood.

Between window and fireplace stood a massive table,
covered for the most part by a cloth, on which the essentials
of every meal were constantly available; sauces, condi-
ments, butter and bread, mustard, pickles, a big square
cheese dish, large cups on a tray, milk, sugar, honey and
jam.

Meals were only regular on the days when Daisy 'did',
otherwise there was no set pattern and they were taken as
and when time allowed.

I had been a guest on 'Daisy's day', back in the autumn,
when I had carried out the annual Tuberculin Test for the
Ministry of Agriculture. It had taken all day, as the cattle
were scattered over the farm and had to be brought in
groups to the buildings.

At one o'clock, we left off testing for the meal. But such was the magnitude of the dinner that I personally found it more of a gastronomic endurance test.

Daisy 'dished up', working noisily between the small enamel cooker, a brownstone sink and a scrubbed, wooden work top in front of the great window. When ready, she turned with a flourish that lacked only a fanfare of trumpets, and advanced upon the table, bearing in each hand a large steaming plateful of her 'plain cookin'.

The presentations resembled volcano-like structures of potato, swede, cabbage and beef, from the craters of which erupted thick, glutinous gravy, flowing downwards in uneven streams.

A knowledge of how to attack such a pile of food was a distinct advantage, for any period of indecision allowed the gravy to swamp everything, congeal and act as a plastic cover to the mound. Picking at it was demoralising, for little impression could be made and, instead of reducing the edifice, it often appeared to increase in size.

Reg and Harry, however, had long mastered the art of attack. They used the element of surprise, known in military circles as the 'pincer' movement. Armed with bent forks and knives, sharpened so often that they were the shape of daggers and possessed the keenness of scalpels, they came from behind.

With their stock-coated arms lying flat upon the tablecloth, encircling their plates, they worked steadfastly away at the distant slopes, drawing closer to their faces as the demolition progressed. Often, they would talk as they ate, a feat that I found absolutely impossible, and, for my part, the whole affair was a challenge to finish, let alone keep up or chat.

For the brothers, 'Daisy's day' was a chance to lay in store until she came again and, despite the vast proportions of the feast, they still cut large slices of bread to accompany it.

There followed plums and custard and great cups of

sweet tea and for the rest of the day I had great difficulty in
bending.

Fortunately, however, there was no feast that night, the
Camp coffee and Haig being a more than admirable substitute.

As I lay back in the armchair, my eye ran over the oak-
beamed, smoke-tarnished ceiling that sported a variety of
iron hooks and brackets, of which only two were in use.
From one hung a large ham, partly wrapped in brown paper;
from the other, a sculptured portion of fat bacon was secured
by a rope running down the wall, which, when released,
caused the bacon to be lowered to slicing height, just above
the table.

Two twelve-bores rested alongside the beam at one end
and an ancient fly paper, black with old victims, adorned
the other.

To the right of the door stood a Welsh dresser. Its shelves
held oddments of blue-and-white china, assorted torches
and battery lamps, pill bottles, keys and several odd-
coloured tins. Cups and mugs commemorating national
anniversaries and coronations hung from the hooks, except
where thick wedges of receipts and invoices were impaled.

Behind the table and running the length of it, against the
wall, was another mighty wooden structure—a black oak
settle. It looked and was the peak of discomfort, for on
sitting, to lean forward was to fall off and to lean back, was
to induce vertigo.

Above the settle and in pride of place, hung the tapestry.

Between the 'dining end' and the 'lounge area', was a
door that led to the rest of the rambling farmhouse, a much
peppered dartboard affixed to its panelling.

Completing the scene, without detracting from the
general spartan atmosphere, was the flagstone floor; some
oddshaped remnants of coconut matting, once colourful,
now sadly worn, made forlorn attempts to soften its un-

charitable face.

Despite the somewhat bare and uninviting appearance, the combination of warmth, the Haig and the night's exertions were making me feel distinctly drowsy. I decided Diana and I had better make a move.

I was about to rise from the armchair when the sound of a labouring engine, a squeak of brakes followed by the slam of a car door, announced Reg's return from the 'Shoes.

The foxy sheepdog, hitherto concealed in the darkness beneath Harry's chair, slid across the floor, sinking expectantly before the kitchen door.

As it opened, a red, smiling face rounded the gap, followed by the rest of Reg, sporting his 'skittlin' clothes—Harris tweed jacket and cap to match, thick pullover, open-necked shirt, twill trousers and large shiny boots.

'Yer can come in . . . the work's done!' said Harry sarcastically.

Reg completely ignored the remark as he continued into the room, brushing aside the foxy dog with his left boot. Then, in one smooth action, as of a man who had definitely got his eye in, his left hand slid the cap from his head and floated it through the air a good twenty feet, to settle on a hook on the opposite wall, while his right hand smoothed some wandering strands of hair over his balding scalp.

Still smiling, he removed his jacket and sank into an armchair, flattening his coat across his knees.

'Well, Hugh. This ain't a social call, I'll be bound,' he said, giving me a broad wink.

'We 'ad trouble with Plum . . . we 'ad to do a Caesar,' interjected Harry nonchalantly.

'All right, Hugh?' asked Reg.

'Mother and son doing well,' I assured.

'An' who be this, then?' Reg smiled at Diana. 'Yer young lady?'

'Yes,' replied Harry, again before I could say anything, 'and 'er kindly give us a hand, too.'

43

Diana smiled, but her eyelids were heavy and she vainly attempted to suppress a yawn.

'Please to meet you, miss.' Reg sat up rather formally, as if suddenly realising there was a lady present.

'I think it's time I took my assistant home,' I said, standing up and stretching. 'Harry can fill you in with the details, Reg. I'll call round tomorrow and check her over.'

'Can we have one peep at her, before we go?' asked Diana.

'I thought you were tired,' I said.

'Just one peep,' she pleaded.

We all trooped across the yard to the loose-box, foxy dog as well, slowly opened the door and peered inside.

The little calf was trying to stand.

Of all the miracles of nature, and there are many—young birds flying, children talking, froglets swimming, even humble liver fluke climbing blades of grass—there is none more dramatic or incomprehensible than a new-born calf attempting to stand for the very first time.

Without instruction book, experience or mechanical aid, it usually achieves its objective within an hour of its arrival into the world. And Plum Five's calf was making a most determined effort.

Initially, in tiny bovines, the design appears all wrong, the weight being apparently greater at the front and the centre of gravity too high. The supports, all four of them, themselves having four joints that work in opposite directions, seem far too gangling and unco-ordinated to be of any use at all.

Even more incongruous is the fact that the soles of the hooves that make up the basal area to receive the whole of the body weight, are softpointed and, compared with the total size of the calf, minuscule.

I'm sure that if Plum's new-born son had realised all this, he would never have attempted the feat in the first place.

'Steady, little chap,' said Diana softly as, like a wound-up toy, he rose shakily out of the straw. His rump partly elevated, he quivered for a few seconds, then toppled forward onto his side. Plum watched benevolently while her offspring heaved and struggled, rather like a battered boxer trying to beat the count.

' 'E'll make it next time,' said Harry.

And shakily, though not very surely, the little bull stood. There was a round of applause and cries of 'Well done!' and, as if he appreciated our concern, he opened his tiny muzzle and gave out a watery 'Baawh!'

' 'E'll do,' said Reg, confidently.

'Marvellous,' said Diana, taking my arm. 'Absolutely marvellous.'

She closed her eyes as I drove back to Ledingford. When we arrived at her house, I gently woke her.

'Coming in?' she asked.

'No,' I said. 'I think some sleep is called for.'

'Oh, Hugh,' she said, 'what a wonderful day.'

And when I finally crawled into bed, I thought it had been pretty wonderful, too.

☆   ☆   ☆

Plum Five died three days later.

When I had visited her on the day following the operation, she had seemed quite well; the wound was clean and she had eaten some meal and a small amount of hay.

The calf was very active and revelled in the sheer joy of its new-found motion by leaping about, flexing and extending its legs and wriggling its short, woolly tail. I had given Plum a brief internal examination and was pleased to find the after-birth had all been discharged. After inserting two pessaries and giving an intramuscular injection of penicillin, I was satisfied all was well.

Reg and Harry were extremely pleased and I told them

that if Plum's recovery continued as well as it had started, I wouldn't need to call again until it was time to remove the skin sutures, some ten days hence.

It was three-thirty in the morning of the following Friday that the telephone in the digs jangled into life.

It penetrated gleefully into my slumbers and received immediate recognition, for time had now conditioned my reactions. Instead of remaining unaware of the signal and relying on Brad to wake me, I responded automatically.

To dreamers not attuned to night calls, a telephone bell can be interpreted in many ways—sleigh bells in the snow, church bells across a meadow, handbells, ship's bells, distant alpine cow bells. But to me, as to any other vet on night call, it was no picturesque illusion—it was a ruddy telephone bell, and no mistake.

Occasionally I tried to ignore it, hoping it would go away . . . but it never did. So, groping for the light switch, I descended the stairs, holding the banister rail, eyes still closed, down to the hall.

'Four-nine-four,' I mumbled.

'That you, Hugh?'

I grunted a reply.

'Hugh, 'Arry 'ere . . . from Wormcastle. Sorry to ring you now, but Plum's a bit rough.'

I rubbed my eyes and shook my head in an attempt to clear the sleep from my mind.

' 'Er 'asn't eaten a thing all day,' Harry went on. 'So, come five o'clock I cut a cabbage from the garden, thinkin' to 'tice 'er a bit . . . but no, she wouldn't touch it. She was breathin' a bit sharp, so I fetched Reg. 'E said there weren't much to be done, that it could be a bit of pain and you'd given her an injection to stop any inflammation. Well, about ten, I looked in on 'er and she was very quiet, standing with 'er 'ead down, and there was a little grunt she was givin'. Ever so soft it was, but a little grunt. I seen 'er again at

46

midnight, an' she was gruntin' 'ard by then, an' I was for callin' you. But Reg said leave 'er till mornin'.'

'But I just been in now, an 'er's bad, Hugh.' I heard Harry swallow and his voice became strained. ' 'Er's down an' gruntin' an' I can't get 'er up, no way!'

By then, I was wide awake.

'Is she flat out?' I asked.

'Yes, lying on 'er right side.'

'Prop her up with some bales,' I ordered, 'and I'll be out straight away.'

Then it was back upstairs two at a time.

Roll-necked pullover over pyjama top, socks on, pyjama bottoms tucked in, trousers on. *En route* through the hall, I grabbed my duffle and out of the pocket plucked a woolly cap, one of the several I possessed, knitted for me by my Aunt Min in Abergranog, who must have thought I wore out one a month, for she kept sending regular batches and I hadn't the heart to refuse.

Wellington boots at the back door, oversocks inside.

Out of the car. Stop. Think.

'Have I got everything?'

A quick mental check of all that I might need and, satisfied that all was on board, I set off in the little Ford for Wormcastle.

Once off the main Brecon road, I pushed on fast through the narrow, winding lanes, my lights swathing along the sprouting hedgerows, flushing out the country night-life. Startled owls, streaking shrews and frozen rabbits flashed by the screen. But my mind was fully occupied with poor Plum, trying to fathom what had gone wrong. What could it be? What could it be? A breakdown of internal sutures, perhaps . . . haemorrhage? Shouldn't be calcium or magnesium deficiency, not in a heifer anyway. I just couldn't understand it, for, forty-eight hours previously, she had looked so well.

The operation had been straightforward, apart from

47

having to hold the womb up to the incision, and all the instruments were accounted for.

What could it be?

Into the yard I charged, round the barn and right up to the loose-box door. The light was shining from inside and, as I made towards it, Reg confronted me.

'It's too late. I think she's gone,' he said.

'She's still breathin' . . . She ain't gone yet!' came Harry's frantic cry from behind him.

I barged past Reg to find Harry kneeling by Plum's head, his hand resting on her horn.

'She did just breathe,' he said, looking up at me sadly.

But, it must have been her last . . . for despite my desperate efforts to support the lungs by compressing the ribs, Plum Five's eyes glazed, her body relaxed, little frothy bubbles appeared in her nostrils and she was dead.

Unexpected death is like a punch in the stomach.

There is always a silence, a realisation of man's inadequacy. What can be said, anyway? No words, signs or actions can ease the initial shock. For seconds, minutes, even longer, one feels nothing.

Then, when the stark finality of the situation dawns, somebody says something; often words of no account . . .

'You can't win 'em all,' said Harry, still on his knees, staring at the floor. Then he looked up at me, as if he knew that I wasn't convinced. 'You can't, Hugh. You can't.'

I turned away and gazed up at the oak-beamed, cobwebbed roof and took a deep breath. It had happened before; it would happen again. But always, no matter how tough and impersonal one tried to be . . . it hurt. 'Okay,' I told myself. 'It was only a cow.'

But still, it hurt.

Then, as in all dramas, the curtain rose again and we went into the next act. I bent forward and reflected Plum's flaccid eyelids . . . the membranes were snow-white.

'Haemorrhage!'

'Bled to death!' blurted Harry.

'Why?' I said, bitterly, 'Why?'

It was Reg, standing by the door, who changed the thinking.

'What are we goin' to do with him?'

I looked at the little bull, fast asleep in the straw, oblivious of all that had passed, still to discover that he was now an orphan.

'Got a cow to put him on?'

'There's Dowager. 'Er lost 'ers last week.'

'Doubt it,' Harry tilted his cap to scratch his greying head. 'She's a mean old bitch . . . kick 'is eye out, more an' like!'

'Put 'im in the pen for tonight,' decided Reg, 'he won't need anything till mornin'.' Then he put his hand on my shoulder. 'Drink of summat, Hugh?'

'No thanks,' I said. 'I'll be getting back, Reg. There's no doubt it's haemorrhage, but God knows from where . . . I don't. I'll see her when she's opened. Where are you sending her?'

'Kennels.'

'Ask them to ring when she's ready. I'd like to know.'

The sooner away, the better. Not that Reg and Harry were in any way reproachful or critical. Country men they were, knew nature's game well and played it by the rules, but I didn't want to stop with them, for I felt sad and hollow and was best alone for a while.

I drove back to Ledingford quite slowly, the trite phrases of self-manufactured condolence swirling about in my mind:

'These things happen.'

'Don't worry about it.'

'You can't win them all.'

Then the doubt crept in: Where did I slip up? Did I slip up . . . Was it my fault?

I had just got to the outskirts of the town, when I remembered.

God! Diana! I thought.

How was she going to take it?

By the time I picked her up from work the following evening, I knew the cause of death. I had been to the kennels and carried out a full *post mortem* examination.

The haemorrhage was the result of an atheroma of the aorta, a rupture of the major artery, an unusual condition in a comparatively young animal.

Plum had 'blown a vessel' as the kennelman put it.

But Diana still took it very badly and for a while kept insisting it was her fault.

'It was nobody's fault,' I tried to tell her. 'In fact, it's a wonder Plum even survived carrying the calf, with such a weak artery. With that sort of deformity, she could have gone any time.'

I put my arm around her. Diana had had her first taste of the harsh paradox of country practice.

4

In the early days, I had shared the digs with Charlie Love, the cheerful Cockney butcher, but after he moved to Chester, where his boss was setting up another shop, I had the place to myself.

Brad still mothered me, airing my clothes if they were damp and even if they were not, insisting constantly that I 'wrap up warm' and scolding me if she thought I was over-working.

Diana often joked that she was worried about taking me on, after the way dear old Brad had fussed over me for so long, and I had to admit that I enjoyed every bit of the attention.

It was with mixed feelings, therefore, that I greeted the news that there was to be another lodger.

'He's a doctor,' Brad announced proudly, 'and wants to stay for a few weeks. It'll be nice for you, Hugh. You'll be able to talk about operations and things.'

Her idea, however, didn't really appeal to me. Apart from losing her undivided attention, I felt that I would no longer be able to shut off the medical side of my life when I came in from work.

That night, I met McBean for a drink in the Hopman Arms and told him about it.

'Where's this fellow from?' he enquired.

'Brad didn't say,' I replied. 'All she knows is that he's a doctor and wants to stay in Ledingford for a while.'

'Well, now, if he's a city chap,' commented McBean, 'he'll find doctoring a mite different in these parts from what he's

51

used to, so he will.' He drank deeply from his pint. 'It's not that far removed from dear old Ireland,' he remarked, smoothing down his moustache.

'Before I came across,' he went on wistfully, in the manner of someone who has been converted to a different religion, 'I was in practice in Kerry, for a short while, just after I qualified, you know. Worked for a fellow called Barney O'Brien. Horse country it was, but good experience at that. I remember coming in one day after a particularly exasperating session with one of those females who thought she knew more about horses than the Good Lord who made the creatures. You know the sort?' McBean indulged in another formidable quaff of his beer and I nodded in agreement, for I was already acquainted with the breed.

' " Barney," I says,' Mac continued, ' " how the divil do you manage these horsey women?"

' "Mac, me boy," he says to me, looking me straight in the eye, "you're a good lad, an' I'll tell you the secret. You've got to get on top of 'em, right from the beginning!" '

McBean slapped his thigh heartily. 'An' d'ye know what I thought, Hugh?' he grinned, mischievously. 'I thought, if that's what vetting is all about down here . . . I'm off. If that's the game, I'll go where there's a bit more talent. So I upped an' came to Ledingford!' McBean stared into his half-empty glass.

'Now, where was I? Ah, yes! Doctoring. One day I was down in Kerry, on a farm, looking at some beasts, and the farmer says to me: "Will you take a look at this?" And, bending his head, he showed me the biggest carbuncle on the back of his neck that I'd ever seen in my life. As big as a mole tump, it was. "What shall I be doing with it?" he asked. "Take it to your doctor and get him to lance it," I said, for it was a fearsome thing and causing him a deal of pain.' McBean paused to refresh himself.

'Well, I was over at his place a few days later; still the poor fellow was hanging his head and I could see the carbuncle was as bad as ever.

' "Did you not get the doctor to lance it?" I said.

' "Sure an' I did," he said.

' "Why is it still as bad?" I said.

' "Failed to do it," the old fellow replied. "Tried several times, hard, so he did. But each time, he kept fallin' off his horse!" '

A smile spread across McBean's face, gradually widening to a broad grin; then he thumped the table, rattling the pints, and dissolved into peals of laughter, and I knew that once again, I had been the victim of his Irish humour.

But in spite of his tall stories and casual manner, Ignatius McBean was a good friend to me in those early days, guiding and advising whenever a difficult situation occurred and always ready to bend an ear to my moans and problems.

☆ ☆ ☆

Doctor Withiel Honeybourne arrived on the Friday evening. I got back about six and was met in the hall by Brad.

'He's in there,' she said, motioning, quite excitedly, towards the living-room. 'Seems a nice sort of man.'

The Doctor was standing with his back to me when I entered, looking at the photograph on the sideboard of Brad's fiancée, the one taken of him in uniform, before his ship was torpedoed in the Atlantic during the War.

He turned and I held out my hand.

'Doctor Honeybourne . . . I presume.' The last two words slipped out, a Freudian slip, perhaps, for I had no intention of trying to appear humorous.

'That is so,' he said. 'And I suppose, in a way, I am a bit of an explorer.'

He smiled and nodded his head and kept nodding gently,

rather like the hinged statuettes popular in the 'thirties. He was certainly much older than I had expected and, unlike most city medical men, his manner was in no way brusque and enquiring.

His hair was an abundant silver-grey his complexion soft, his features gentle. The dark, double-breasted suit he wore was of a medical style and, as he removed his glasses, which were devoid of earpieces and attached to his waistcoat by a black cord, rather like pince-nez, he reminded me of the Reverend Deri Jones at Abergranog Baptist Chapel.

I wondered if Doctor Honeybourne ever copied the old minister's trick of wrinkling his nose when he had finished reading, allowing the glasses to cascade down his jacket, arrested, just in time, by the safety cord. But he was much smaller in stature than the Reverend Deri and his voice softer—no comparison with the 'fire and brimstone' volume of the old Welsh cleric.

'Hugh Lasgarn,' I said, as we shook hands. 'Brad says you're staying for a few weeks.'

'Yes,' he replied, his head still nodding gently. 'And you are a veterinary surgeon, I believe?'

'Yes,' I said. 'General practice.' Then, without trying to appear too inquisitive, I asked: 'And what is your speciality?'

'Old relics and the like,' he replied.

'Geriatrics?'

'No,' he said, smiling. 'The deader they are, the more interesting I find them.'

'Oh, pathology!' I exclaimed.

'No,' he replied, 'mediaeval history.'

There could have been no greater contrast than the characters of Charlie Love and Doctor Honeybourne, yet both of them provided me with an insight into life that was decidedly beneficial.

Charlie, extrovert, happy-go-lucky, cheeky, chatty and outrageous in his dress, taught me to enjoy and appreciate the present; Doctor Honeybourne epitomised the genteel intellectual, having spent most of his life up at Oxford, researching, studying and lecturing about the subject he loved so dearly. He instilled into me an interest, and indeed a respect, for things of the past.

I often wondered how the two would have got on, had they both been at Brad's at the same time. It would have been a most absorbing encounter.

Doctor Honeybourne had retired from the University and was taking the opportunity to follow up some of his more peripheral interests.

'Most of my life has been involved with the Dark Ages,' he told me, 'and, now that I have time, I decided to modernise my outlook and advance as far as the lighter shadows of the nineteenth century. I suspect that the daylight of present times would be too traumatic an experience for someone of my years.

'The Reverend Francis Kilvert, eighteen-forty to eighteen seventy-nine,' he added, lapsing into a donnish preoccupation with historical detail, 'has always held a particular fascination for me.

'Apart from his literary merit, his Diaries have pictured so faithfully life of all kinds in the country parishes hereabout, during what some regard and, I might say, erroneously in my opinion—'then he wrinkled his nose and, to my amusement, demonstrated Pastor Deri's mannerism of allowing his glasses to tumble downwards—'erroneously, as the "good old days".

'For an historian,' he continued, resiting his specs, 'who has spent a lifetime trying to imagine the atmosphere generated by ancient peoples, Kilvert's Diaries are exciting to me, since most of the inns, churches and country mansions he frequented are still readily recognisable. And because the people who loved, laughed, married and died in those houses are not so long departed, I hope that the 'feel' of history will be that much more perceptible.'

How I enjoyed listening to the learned old gentleman; indeed, it was my acquaintance with Doctor Honeybourne that led to my own interest in the Reverend Francis Kilvert, for a considerable portion of the Hacker practice, including Wormcastle, lay in Kilvert country.

The 'feel' for the past, as Doctor Honeybourne so aptly described it, made all the difference to my appreciation of the present; it gave a new dimension to my work on the ancient farmsteads and estates.

I took particular interest in the rural architecture and became fascinated by such objects as mouldy leather horse collars, the straw poking through the rotten linings, or toothless hay rakes, flails and broken forks, wondering who was the last person to hang them on the hook or leave them, bent and worm-eaten, in some forgotten corner.

Francis Kilvert, I discovered, was quite a legend. Born in 1840 at Hardenhuish, near Chippenham, where his father was rector of the parish, he completed his education at Oxford, where he studied at Wadham, which may have explained Doctor Honeybourne's affinity with the rural diarist. In 1862 he obtained his B.A., and his M.A. four years later, in 1866.

He became curate of Clyro, just up the River Wye, remaining there for seven years. After a short time, back home in his native Wiltshire, he returned to Herefordshire and the Wye Valley, and a living at St Harmon's, but eventually came to Bredwardine in 1877.

Of course, the 'good old days' were only good for some, as Doctor Honeybourne rightly surmised, and the Reverend Francis Kilvert, being a 'man of the cloth', was a well accepted figure in all walks of life in the parish.

Consequently, his social graces and parochial duties took him into both local mansions and the lowliest cottages, where he observed human nature in all its guises.

Humanitarian, with a sincere love of people and a detestation of any form of violence, he also delighted in the surrounding beauty of the countryside, walking as far as the distant Black Mountain and even beyond, to Llanthony and into Wales.

Life must have seemed idyllic to the respected and well-loved country parson; but I often thought, when reading his works, that although one could easily deplore the weakening of clerical influence, it was difficult to forget the cap-touching and servility of those times and the gulf that separated the fortunate from the majority.

Even the livestock didn't have it so good, and the 'lowing herd, winding slowly o'er the lea' of Gray's *Elegy in a Country Churchyard*, which I well remembered from my School Certificate days, was probably riddled with tuberculosis, mastitis and abortion.

Distance lends enchantment to the view and, for my part, despite my fascination with Kilvert's era, I was glad to be a country vet in the twentieth century, rather than a horse doctor several decades before.

Doctor Honeybourne intended to follow in the tracks of the reknowned cleric and, on the day of his first excursion, I was mildly amused at the transformation from learned don to intrepid explorer.

He wore tweed plus-fours and steel-capped walking boots, with a green eyeshade on his head to protect him against the sun. Over one shoulder he carried a haversack containing a pork pie, sandwiches and a flask of china tea, which Brad had prepared; whilst over the other hung a camera, complete with filters—orange for mountain, yellow for sky. These accoutrements, together with a compass, tripod, walking stick, police whistle and most incongruous of all, a fly whisk, he loaded into his tiny Standard Eight and set off down the winding pathways that would lead him back in time.

For me, however, it was to be a very different day, the occasion, in fact, on which I received my first serious patient-inflicted injury.

Prior to this unfortunate event, I had received the usual minor traumas experienced in veterinary work, such as bumps and kicks from cows and horses.

'The closer you be, the less it 'urts,' Harry Bayne had informed me one day, after I had been put on my back by a miserable old Hereford who was so quick and accurate that she could kick you a second time upon the same spot, before you had even felt the first. To my mind, his advice was a load of rubbish—it 'urt', wherever you stood.

My previous most 'urtful' encounter had involved the knuckle of my right index finger, which had been ground between the molars of another wretched Hereford cow, whose mouth I was attempting to investigate.

It was my own fault, I was in too much of a hurry and scorned the use of the aluminium Drinkwater's gag (used to jam the jaws apart). I thought I could prevent the teeth closing upon my hand by holding the patient's tongue out of the side of her mouth, relying upon the principle that, before she could bite me, she would bite herself—and my hand would be safe.

But tongues are slippery things, especially foot-long, bovine specimens, and, as I pursued my examination, I lost my grip, leaving me standing with my hand completely unprotected, halfway down the patient's throat.

The Hereford cow looked at me spitefully before she bit and, not content with a simple chop, she moved her jaws from side to side, so that my knuckle was ground between the irregular, spiky tables of her dentures. The pain was excruciating and my finger was badly swollen for several days. But even worse were the ribald comments I had to suffer regarding my bandaged right index finger! However, I sought no medical attention for my injury, which resolved spontaneously in a couple of weeks.

On the fateful day of my more serious injury, I had taken a call to visit Mr Molson at the Rhyde, near Brackhope.

The Rhyde was a small, isolated estate, deep amid woodland and more reminiscent of a settlement than a farm, for the buildings were mostly wooden and seemed of a somewhat temporary nature. Perhaps the fact that the owner was a retired tea-planter may have had something to do with it.

I rarely met him in person, but often caught sight of him sitting in a rocking chair on the porch of his bungalow-type residence, regardless of the weather, probably imagining he was still amid the Blue Mountains or some other far-flung outpost.

There were some detached living huts, also of wood, situated on the perimeter of the estate, which housed several gypsy families that bred hordes of barefooted children and lurcher dogs.

The gypsies and their womenfolk worked for Mr Molson, or 'Master' as they called him, either in the hop-yard, tending the stock or in the fields. One sensed a certain tribal atmosphere about the place, as if the old gentleman's colonial influence persisted, in some degree, even in deepest Herefordshire.

There were twenty Ayrshire cows in the small dairy herd and about the same number of cross-bred bullocks which were fattened; a flock of Ryeland sheep; some goats; assorted barnyard fowl—and one pig.

It was the pig that I had been asked to see.

There was, however, something very special about this pig. It belonged to Mrs Molson, a large, red-faced lady who paraded about the estate wearing a voluminous floral dress, a straw hat and wellington boots.

The sow was the pride, joy, pet and companion of the dear lady, who spent all her time cleaning, caressing and

59

generally caring for the pampered porker. Its name was Umtali—which had some African significance known only to Mrs Molson—and it lived in grand style in a cot at the back of the bungalow, well away from common creatures.

Umtali had been delivered, two days previously, of ten healthy piglets; but, following the arrival of her family, she had refused to move other than occasionally to her trough, where she sniffed at the delicacies laid before her, picked at a few morsels, took a little drink, then, like some cosseted prima-donna taking to her bed, lay down in the straw and sulked.

Mrs Molson was obviously distressed and very concerned as she described Umtali's condition, talking of her pet as if she were quite human.

'I stayed with her all night, mopping her brow constantly as she went through the labour,' she explained. 'Oh, Mr Lasgarn, how she did suffer.' Mrs Molson sighed deeply, so that her bosom caused the floral dress to shiver frantically. Then she clasped her hands and added emotionally: 'If I could have had them for her, I would!'

When I entered the cot, the piglets scurried into a corner, falling over each other in an attempt to bury themselves in a huddle amid the straw. Umtali, meanwhile, lay against the far wall, asleep and softly snoring, a troughful of porcine delectables untouched before her.

I closed the half-door behind me lest the piglets should escape, and studied my patient.

Umtali's breathing rate was fifteen per minute, about normal for her condition. I took a closer look at her skin for the tell-tale patches of Swine Erysipelas, but it was clear.

I decided to take her temperature. Opening my case, which I had set down beside me, I took out my thermometer, shook it down and gently inserted it into her rectum. As I waited, on my knees behind the somnolent hulk, I ran my left hand cautiously along her engorged teats to check for mastitis.

'No trouble there,' I announced to Mrs Molson, who had stayed outside but was looking on, most concernedly, over the door.

The temperature was elevated by two degrees, to just over 104°F, and a slight discharge suggested there could be a mild inflammation of the womb—not uncommon in sows, following delivery of a large litter.

Taking my stethoscope, I examined Umtali's great hairy chest for signs of pneumonia, but despite the sonorous drone, I found her air passages to be clear.

After due consideration, I decided the problem must be uterine.

'I'll give her an injection to control the bacteria,' I informed Mrs Molson. 'That should do the trick all right.'

After preparing the syringe with penicillin, I gently inserted the needle through the skin behind Umtali's left ear and injected the drug.

She never budged.

'Wish all my patients took their shots as well as that,' I commented as, still kneeling beside the great sow, I put away my syringe and closed the case. 'Well done, old lady, I'm sure you'll feel a lot better tomorrow.' And as I rose, I slapped her heartily on the buttocks.

Umtali opened one eye. It was the first time she had shown any interest in the proceedings. Then she closed it again.

But somewhere in her tiny porcine brain something had fused, for two seconds later she opened her beady eye again . . . then raised her head. In a flash she was up, turning and, jaws apart, came straight at me, screaming hysterically.

I was caught in the act of straightening up from my kneeling position and fenced off her first attack with my case. But she came like a battering ram, my action only serving to steady her momentarily.

Then she charged again, and this time scored a direct hit.

I had recently bought a pair of three-quarter thigh boots for work; 'trawler-men's' boots they were called, being rather like extended wellingtons but not as long as waders. The knee-pieces were of reinforced rubber, for leaning against the fishing boat rails when hauling in the nets.

Full protection though they might have given against groaning spars in a Force Ten in the North Sea, they were no match for Umtali on the rampage, and she sank her razor-sharp tusks through the thickened rubber and deep into my thigh. Then, lifting her head sharply, she ripped a long gash.

I shall never know how I got out.

Mrs Molson, who knew a lot about ballet and had seen some of the greatest performances, said later that it was the finest leap she had ever witnessed. But as far as I was concerned, the aestheticism of my exit was the least of my cares—all I know is, I came over that door like a rocket, case and all.

Mrs Molson was most apologetic.

'You shouldn't be so naughty when kind Mr Lasgarn was just trying to make you feel better,' she scolded her pride and joy, but as I hobbled back to my car, rather stronger reprimands were going through my mind.

As I turned the little Ford in the yard, Mrs Molson approached my open window, to say once more how sorry she was. The pain in my leg was intensifying, but it was the dear, ex-colonial lady's final remarks that left me speechless.

'Of course,' she added, glancing at the floor and nodding her straw-hatted head, as if the thought had just struck her, 'perhaps I should have told you. You see, I'm the only one who ever deals with Umtali. She absolutely hates men!'

Because of the rigidity of the rubber boot-top, I was still unaware of the extent of my wound, but about a mile from the Rhyde, at Hope Wood, I stopped to investigate the damage. When I got out and removed the boot, I found my trouser leg soaked in blood and a split in the material revealed a six-inch gash in my thigh. I was surprised at the depth of it, for due to the commotion there had been relatively little pain. But as I studied it, my leg started to throb and I realised my wound would need some stitches, so I high-tailed it for the General Hospital.

The doctor who stitched me up thought it was all a huge joke.

'Thought the only difference between doctors and vets, these days, was that you still eat your patients,' he exclaimed jovially as he needled away. 'Never thought of your patients eating you!'

However, Diana and Brad gave me a lot of sympathy, which was very gratifying and McBean and Bob Hacker were also very concerned.

The only other casualty of the affair, for which I felt personally sorry, was my medical bag, the one that had belonged to Hacker Senior and that Bob, his son, had given to me after his father's death. It was still usable, but the leather cover bore a long scar, resulting from Umtali's first, violent sortie.

I apologised to Bob about it, but he smiled and said:

'When I gave you that case, Hugh, I said the old man would open the right drawers for you—but as well as that, he's helping you to hold it in the right place, too.'

And when I thought it over, I realised that had it not been for that case, the whole incident could have done a young country vet, soon to be married, a lot of harm . . . in more ways than one!

☆   ☆   ☆

There was no denying it, I had been frightened by Umtali. Not through cowardice, but because of the unpredictability of the situation. Yet it had been a lesson and nothing to be ashamed of, for I came to accept that being frightened was very much a part of rural practice.

The horse that might kick, the dog that might bite, the sow that might charge, produced in me a sharpening of the senses, an awareness of the situation without which a country vet, like a bat without its radar, would not last very long.

Fear is the emotion that creates the greatest impact on the human mind. To be frightened is a transient, physiological reaction to an adverse situation, but true fear leaves a scar on the subconscious, like the mark on my leather case, that can never be erased.

The realisation of the psychological gulf between fright and fear was to come to me later—in fact, several years later and many miles from the rich, gentle Herefordshire countryside.

Despite Umtali's temperamental outburst, I soon regained my confidence and put her attitude down to the fact that she was being a bloody-minded female. Once again, whilst I was no chauvinist, I was aware that there were differences between male and female, other than just the physical variations.

Of course, even physical differences could cause complications, as they did in another porcine problem in which I was involved.

As well as long-established yeoman farmers, our clients spanned the social strata with great variety. There were ex-colonials like Mr Molson, retired industrialists, judges, artists and also a considerable number of 'Army men'.

One of whom was Colonel Phippson.

It was a Thursday afternoon. McBean had taken the only two farm calls, Bob Hacker had gone fishing and I was sitting at his desk, writing up the results of a Tuberculosis Test for the Ministry.

After each test, the forms had to be completed with the individual animal's ear number, which was either a tattoo in the pedigrees or metal tags in others; the breed description, signified by 'H' for Hereford, 'F' for Friesian, 'SH' for Shorthorn and so on (crossbreds were entered as 'Hx' or 'Fx'); the age, in months or years, and the sex. Each piece of information had a separate box of its own.

The vital statistics were the skin readings, measured in millimetres—red for the top of the neck, where the avian tuberculin was injected, and black for the lower neck, where bovine tuberculin was injected. Firstly the readings before the tuberculin, which was the sensitising agent consisting of a harmless extract of dead tuberculosis germs: about 5 to 7mm in the light breeds and 9 to 15mm in the heavier beef breeds; some of the Hereford bulls recorded skin measurements of 20 and 25mm. Then the readings taken 72 hours later, when any increase in skin thickness was recorded and placed in its appropriate box.

A description of the type of swelling was next required, which could be 'c', 'so', 'do' or 'eo', standing for circumscribed, slight oedema, diffuse oedema or extensive oedema; oedema being the fluid reaction in the skin.

Again, every entry referring to an avian or top reaction was entered with a red pen and every bovine one with a black pen.

Finally, the result. If there was no difference in the initial and test measurements, a negative sign, in the appropriate red or black, was scored. If the reaction exceeded the original by two millimetres, it was doubtful and an 'O' was scored; but if the reaction was greater than four, it was a positive result and a large 'plus' sign was inserted in the relevant box and, of course, in the correct colour.

Any animal showing an excess of four millimetres of black mammalian reaction over the red avian, was re-tested within one month, whilst a larger increase denoted an animal carrying infection, which was duly removed from the herd and slaughtered.

Filling in the sheets for a large herd could be tedious and

I far preferred to carry out the test than fill in the results. On the farm the readings were taken down in a hardbacked notebook, then transferred to the sheets back at the surgery.

I once protested about this repetition to Bob Hacker and suggested we took the sheets directly onto the farm on a clip-board, filling them in on the spot and thereby saving considerable time.

His reply was very practical. 'A good idea, Hugh,' he said. 'But the problem is keeping it clean and free of contamination under farm conditions—there's enough bullshit on these forms already!'

However, despite all the paper-work, the effects of the Tuberculosis Eradication Scheme were becoming evident, both in the improvement in quality of the livestock and, even more importantly, in the reduction of cases of tuberculosis in humans. It was a health measure invaluable to both public and livestock, for which the Ministry of Agriculture and private veterinary practitioners could claim the major part of the credit.

I was in a state of confusion, trying to add up the numbers and sort out how many heifers, cows, bulls, calves and steers I had tested, when the telephone rang.

It was the sort of 'phone call that immediately made one sit up, straighten the shoulders and clear the mind.

'Colonel Phippson here! Is that the vet?'

I moved the receiver a further two inches from my ear.

'Just moved down here,' continued the Colonel brusquely, not waiting for my reply. 'Went's Hollow, you know. Farming. Small way, of course. Got a few pigs. Tricky things, pigs. Trouble with one of 'em. Could you be a good chap and pop along?'

'What symptoms?' I enquired.

'Rather delicate, old boy. Fill you in when you come!'

Went's Hollow was unrecognisable.

The old, dilapidated smallholding had been occupied, de-briefed, redeployed and probably signed for in triplicate, since the Colonel had taken command. Everything that moved had been picked up and everything that didn't had been whitewashed.

The Colonel, complete with flat cap, combat jacket, thumbstick and moustache, advanced across the yard as I arrived. Behind him and to the right, by three paces, trotted his wife, combat-jacketed, tweed-skirted, gum-booted, her face obscured by the great knot that secured her tightly drawn headscarf.

'Glad you made it, Lasgarn!' He held out his hand, his gesture absolving me from any decision about saluting. We shook palms vigorously, I acknowledged his wife and we led 'orf' in single file, in the direction of the thumbstick.

The pig unit was a credit to any outfit, with brushes and buckets lined up, in order of size. Meal bags stood to attention in the corner, a large NO SMOKING sign plastered on the wall above them.

'Here!' he motioned over the top of a pen. 'Two so far. Young females. Trouble with that one!' He nodded his flat cap towards a sparkling Large White, nuzzling away in the corner. 'Swelling beneath her tail. See?'

I appraised the situation, gathered my thoughts, considered how best to report the facts—and began.

'That's normal, Colonel,' I explained. 'Your gilt is 'brimming', 'on heat', she's ready for the boar. There's always a reaction in that area, when it happens. Usually it occurs every three weeks, until she gets pregnant.'

At this, his lady turned away, with what I assumed was feminine embarrassment.

There followed an uncomfortable pause.

Then, the Colonel's moustache twitched and a grin spread across his face.

'My God!' he exclaimed. 'My wife's been poulticing it for

two days!'

As I drove back to Ledingford, I wondered to myself what the Regiment would have thought. Colonel Phippson was certainly right when he declared pigs to be 'tricky things'. When it came to livestock, 'things' were not always what they seemed.

I remembered McBean describing such an incident that he had attended, on a farm up the Pyon Valley, some two months previously.

A client of ours, by name of Archie Todd, had rung to say he was going up to the Smithfield Show, but was worried about his best sow, due to farrow while he was away.

Apparently she had had trouble at the previous birth and he asked if one of us could call by to check on her while he was in London. His workman, Arnold, was going to keep an eye on things, but was not too reliable, being a bit partial to the local 'scrumpy'.

It was just on dusk, or 'the edge of night' as it was known locally, when McBean visited the farm. He could see a light in the pig cot and made his way over to it.

Leaning over the door, he saw Arnold, fast asleep in the straw, an empty cider flagon beside him and, lying opposite, the great hairy body of Archie Todd's valuable sow.

As McBean looked on, she gave a mighty heave and a little wet, wriggling piglet slipped out into the straw. As with all piglets, it was soon on its feet and searching for the milk bar. As it nosed unsteadily along the great, steaming wastes of the sow's belly, she suddenly raised her head and, to McBean's horror, opened her massive jaws and swallowed the little piglet, like a bullfrog swatting a fly.

McBean's eyes nearly popped from his head and he yelled at the top of his voice: 'Wake up, Arnold! The sow is eating her pigs!' As he did so, another piglet was delivered and appeared destined for the same fate.

Arnold opened his eyes and coughed.

'Wake up!' shouted McBean again. 'Watch that little pig!'

Arnold studied the little pink body for a few moments, then looked up and, with a bleary smile on his reddened face, said:

'Don' you worry, Mr McBean. 'Im's all right. 'Im be just playin'. Doin' it all night 'e 'ave—goin' in the one end an' out the t'other.'

5

There is no substitute for experience—but acquiring the experience can be an experience in itself, and every day brought new twists to the set pattern of diagnostic procedures and standard treatments that I had been taught at University.

Indeed, how much I valued my 'seeing practice' days with C. J. Pink at Newpool, for by using one of his techniques at Little Pentwyn, a small mixed farmstead hidden in the Penarden Woods, I consolidated my reputation in that area. This was mainly due to the fact that Evan Bevan, the owner, who was both forester and farmer, was also the local gas-bag and had a permanent nightly perch on a stool at the Black Lion.

The case was a bullock with a 'chaff' in its eye. Evan, despite all the resources of local witchcraft, had failed to remove it.

In many cases where the vet was called as a last resort, one was on a hiding to nothing and, although most folks were fair and called us early, sometimes half the parish had first been consulted, so that the result was an advanced condition and a weak patient.

To get to Little Pentwyn was a minor expedition in itself, for it lay a mile beyond Pentwyn Court Farm along the forest track.

There were no less than nine gates that had to be opened and closed: one at the road entrance to Pentwyn Court, one at the end of the first field; three at the farm itself, which one had to go through, one at the end of the far field, another at the start of the forest track, the eighth halfway along and the ninth and last at Evan Bevan's yard.

When there was livestock about, it demanded seventy-two 'ins' and 'outs' of the little Ford. Out to open, in to go through, out to shut, then back in to drive to the next—and the same all the way back.

The forest track would have been a formidable course for tank training and, in parts, already appeared to have been used for such a purpose. Indeed, it would never have surprised me to see a ten-ton Churchill come trundling towards me. The deep ruts of the narrow winding trail had been the result of the forest tractor hauling wood, a mudcovered Fordson that, with a full load and belching oily smoke, could in itself look quite frightening.

Stones had been layed in the major pot-holes, but many were odd-shaped and pointed, ready to jab the tyres, bend the track rods or dent the exhaust of any civilised vehicle.

Getting to the far end was like paddling in a bucket to an island, through an exceptionally rough sea.

Evan was leaning on the ninth gate, puffing his pipe, while beside him stood a ferrety little man in an oversize poacher's jacket, breeches, leggings and a flat cap.

They both watched me bumble uncomfortably towards them, but made no attempt to open the gate. Only when I stopped did they show me any recognition, which consisted of Evan lazily waving his arm, indicating that I had pulled up too close to the gate and would have to reverse a yard before he could swing it ajar.

'Hugh Lasgarn' I announced, as I emerged. 'The vet.'

He nodded, while the ferrety one eyed me suspiciously.

'Bullock with a "chaff"?'

Evan Bevan took his pipe from his mouth and blew a balloon of grey smoke in my direction—it was sharp, acidic and made me cough.

'In there, fast,' he commented. 'We can't shift it.'

'What have you tried?' I asked.

'Sugar and salt,' said the ferrety man.

I looked enquiringly at Evan Bevan.

'This is Mr Bowen the Bont,' said Evan. 'Does a bit of doctoring around here. His "sugar an' salt" never failed afore."

I wasn't too sure what he meant, but Evan explained without my asking. 'He blows a bit in an' the eye waters it out, usually—but not this time.'

'Never failed before,' reiterated Bowen the Bont irritably.

I could well imagine why an eye would water with 'sugar and salt' in it, and thought the method a bit barbaric, but decided to leave any criticism until later.

He led off through the yard and, pulling my case from the car, I followed. Bowen the Bont kept his distance behind, like a wary sheepdog.

The yard was muddy and led to the buildings, arranged in two short terraces on either side—the house and barn on the right, and on the left a low cowshed and an open-fronted building containing the Fordson and an ancient mowing machine.

The land behind the house and barn fell away steeply, affording a magnificent view of the valley below.

At the near end of the house, a kitchen of blue corrugated tin had been added, obviously assembled from a collection of builders' oddments, for the door was pink and had a coat hook on the outside, the window was made up of about twenty small panes and the guttering and drainpipe were of cast iron, completely out of proportion to the size of the roof.

A clattering of dishes caught my ear and, through the multi-paned window, I spied a dark-haired, rosy-cheeked girl washing up.

'Want anything?' asked Evan, as we passed the door.

'Soap, towel and water would be handy,' I said.

Evan went to the pink door, which stuck when he first

72

pulled it, but opened at the second attempt.

'Soap, towel and water for the vet!' he shouted to the girl. 'Hazel, my daughter,' he explained, shutting the door and joining me again. 'She'll bring it.'

Then he led the way to the barn.

The bullock was a crossed Hereford, black with a white face and quite large. Evan pushed open a wooden hatch which opened onto the midden. "Ave a bit more light,' he said gruffly, as a shaft of winter sunshine burst through.

Now that the interior was brighter, I could see a pen of calves in the far corner, while in another pen, a bullock quite as large as the first was contentedly munching on some hay.

My patient, however, looked a sorry sight, for its eye was swollen and discharging, obviously the result of the iniquitous 'salt and sugar' treatment. Its only effect had been to leave a long streaky tearstain down the poor beast's white face. Occasionally it jerked its head back sharply in response to the pain it was undoubtedly suffering.

'That "salt and sugar" has made a mess of it,' I said, as I took a closer look. 'I think it's a cruel form of treatment.'

'That's what I told them!' announced a voice behind me. It was Hazel, bearing a bowl of steaming water, soap and a snow-white towel. 'How would you like it in your eye?' she continued, glaring at Bowen the Bont, who shrank back into the shadows at her reprimand, while her father sucked the stem of his pipe.

'Worked afore,' he said sheepishly.

Hazel tossed her head scornfully. 'Here's your water,' she said, putting it down with a thump on the floor.

Then she turned on her heel and left us.

The fact that Bowen had already tampered with the eye had not only caused the lids to become swollen, making an examination of the eye-ball extremely difficult, but the bullock was nervous of any further interference and kept turning its head away.

I got Evan to hold the beast's horn with his right hand,

and steady the head by holding the nose with the other. Then, by rolling the head over as far as possible, the bullock automatically opened the affected eye, in an attempt to see what was going on.

I manoeuvred the head, with Evan's help, into the shaft of sunlight where I could see the eye clearly and, parting the eyelids, I caught sight of a piece of yellow chaff, about half an inch long, lying across the cornea.

'It's stuck pretty firm,' I commented. 'But it will have to come out of there, or your beast will go blind.'

I explained that any foreign body that resisted the normal tear defence could cause serious damage to the surface. It reacted rather like a stone on a frozen pond, gradually sinking into the ice, except that the ice was the corneal surface and the result, ulceration, considerable pain and eventual blindness.

'And how do *you* propose to get it out, Mr Vet?' said Bowen the Bont sarcastically from the shadows.

'With a knife,' I said. 'A sharp knife.'

Evan was visibly disturbed by my remark and his hand tightened on the bullock's horn.

'A knife!' echoed Bowen. 'In the eye? Now ain't that cruel?'

'There'll be an anaesthetic, Mr Bowen,' I replied sharply. 'The bullock will feel no pain.'

With Evan holding the head, I took some local and squirted a few millilitres between the swollen eyelids, then I unwrapped my scalpel handle and fitted a new blade.

'You sure you know what you'm doin'?' asked Evan nervously, as I approached with my shining instrument.

'The principle is to press the knife gently against the surface of the eye,' I explained, not reacting to his lack of confidence, 'and as the eyeball moves, by sliding the blade in the opposite direction I should be able to peel off the "chaff", like a stamp from a letter.'

'Done this afore?' asked Bowen suspiciously.

There was no advantage in telling him that I hadn't, or reminding myself it was the first time, for the job demanded a steady hand—and mine was already quivering.

'Hold him steady and turn him when I say,' I told Evan, and at the same time I heard his pipe-stem crack between his teeth, but he made no comment.

As Evan rotated the head, I rested my clenched hand on the bullock's cheek, with the scalpel poised over the surface of the eye. By pressing against the bullock, I kept a steady hold and slowly lowered the razor sharp edge onto the cornea.

I could see the 'chaff' sitting in the angle of the eyelid, but although the surface flicked back and forth, it didn't budge and came nowhere near my blade.

After three attempts it was still there, and I straightened up to ease my aching back.

'It's pretty firm,' I said.

'We knows that,' retorted Bowen.

Evan made no comment, but his expression was one of doubt and concern.

After castigating the 'sugar and salt' method, I had to make mine work, so I bent down for another attempt.

This time I just tweaked the end of the 'chaff'.

'It's coming,' I announced. 'Bend his head over a bit more.'

He twisted the bullock's head and the eyeball rotated a little further. One more flick and I had loosened it, and at the third attempt it slid onto my knife and I lifted it out triumphantly.

'How about that!' I said, holding the scalpel with the 'chaff' under Bowen the Bont's narrow nose. 'Clean as a whistle!'

'You sure you haven't damaged the eye?' he snapped.

I shook my head. 'It will be as good as new, once the inflammation caused by your "sugar and salt" has subsided.'

'Looks better already,' said Evan, squinting at the bullock's face. 'Clever bit of work, Mr Lasgarn. Eh, Bowen?'

But Bowen the Bont made no comment. 'I'll see you Friday in Hay,' he said to Evan and, without giving me so much as a glance, shuffled out through the door.

'Now you'm 'ere, 'ave a look at these,' said Evan, his tone now more friendly and relaxed. 'They've all got it, look.'

He pointed to the five small calves in the pen. They were a mix of brown and black, some with white faces and some mottled, but every one had round, yellow, crusty patches over the skin.

In some areas, the raised lesions were individual, but others joined to form quite large, hairless lesions on the body.

I moved to one side to let the light shine into the pen, but further examination was unnecessary, for it was obviously Ringworm.

'Bowen made some stuff up for me,' said Evan, holding out a pot of black liquid. 'But if you've anything better, I'd rather 'ave it.'

I smelt Bowen's concoction, which appeared to consist mainly of sump-oil.

'I've got some iodine and glycerine in the car,' I said, 'which should do the trick, but these old buildings will be full of it, so you'll have to watch out for re-infection.'

'We've had it for years,' said Evan. 'Every winter, something gets it. How can I stop it?'

'It's a fungus that grows in the hair roots,' I told him. 'When it's ripe, it forms spores which are very resistant and rub off into the woodwork or the bark of trees, outside. You can creosote or white-lime the walls, but that only kills the surface spores and some of them penetrate quite deeply, so that they are capable of surfacing years later, and causing infection. Lining the walls with tin sheet is a good idea, or you could burn off the surface with a blow-lamp.'

'Don't think I'd risk that,' said Evan, 'Place would go up

like a matchbox.'

Before I left, I put some ointment into the bullock's eye and gave Evan a tube to continue the treatment. 'Come to the car and I'll give you the Ringworm Lotion,' I said, drying my hands on the snow-white towel.

As we passed the kitchen door on the way to the car, Evan turned towards it. 'Just a minute,' he said and, opening the pink door, once again at the second attempt, disappeared inside. A few minutes later he called to me.

'I wonder could you step inside, Mr Lasgarn, and take a look at this?'

He gave no indication what 'this' was, but beckoned me to enter. So, putting down my case, I went into the kitchen.

Hazel was standing by the sink, which was now clear of china and contained some potatoes she was preparing for a meal.

'Show Mr Lasgarn,' said Evan.

And with that, Hazel yanked up her skirt to her waist, revealing a shapely pair of legs and even more shapely thighs.

'What do you think of that!' said Evan.

For once, I was lost for words.

A cheeky smile came over Hazel's face; she was obviously enjoying my embarrassment. 'There!' she said, turning her right thigh slightly outward and nodding her head. 'I've had it a week and it's getting bigger!'

I bent forward to take a closer look, then recoiled a little, lest I appeared too enthusiastic, to examine a circular reddened lesion about the size of a florin, on her pure-white skin.

'What do you think of it, then?' repeated Evan.

'That's Ringworm, too,' I said. 'You probably caught it from the calves. It's highly contagious.'

'That stuff of yourn any good for it?' enquired Evan.

'Mine is for cattle,' I said. 'I couldn't advise it for humans.

77

You'd best see a doctor.'

'No time to go down there,' said Hazel, still holding her skirts well above her waist. 'I'll have to use that mixture Bowen brought.'

'That could make things worse,' I said, 'and your skin might get badly burnt.'

'Just leave some of yours for the calves, then.' said Evan.

'And only for the calves,' I insisted, but from the look on both their faces, I knew what they would do.

I thought of pretending that I hadn't got any in the car after all. But then, the condition in both calves and girl wanted treatment, and glycerine and iodine was not too severe. In fact, it might work well on Hazel, but I couldn't recommend it.

As I trundled back along the forest track, I mused on the fickleness of confidence that clients could hold towards their vet.

On the one hand, doubting my ability to remove a 'chaff' from a bullock's eye; on the other, asking me to treat one of the family.

As I approached the yard gate at Pentwyn Court Farm, I saw John Pitt, the owner, and his son, standing by.

The lad, a tall willowy youth, stepped forward to open the gate and, as I drove through, I stopped to thank him.

When he held back the gate, I noticed his wrist was bandaged.

'Sprain?' I enquired.

'No', he replied. 'Ringworm.'

'Caught it off the cattle?' I asked.

'Our cattle don't have no Ringworm,' snapped his father.

As the gate closed behind me and I pulled away down the track, my mind went back to my parasitology days at Glasgow University and the set pattern of diagnostic procedures and standard treatments.

'Ringworm is a fungus that can survive up to four years

in a suitable environment. It is highly contagious and re-infection can occur from woodwork such as gates, doors and stiles, or even free-living trees such as Elm, Beech, Sycamore and Oak.'

They never mentioned Hazel.

☆   ☆   ☆

I had two more farm visits that afternoon and finished up at the head of the valley. There were two possible routes back to Ledingford, one the way I had come, or alternatively I could cross over the hill and go back along by the river. I was deliberating on the choice at the road junction when my eye caught a signpost leaning backwards in the overgrown hawthorn hedge. Although the writing was weathered and the finger at an angle away from me, I could just pick out the words 'Arthur's Stone'.

The name registered in my mind, for just a few evenings previously, Doctor Honeybourne had been talking about the ancient neolithic tomb.

I remembered being quite taken by the old gentleman's enthusiasm for such an object as a communal burial ground, which was what the cairn signified, that bore the name.

'The final structure,' he expounded, 'appears to have contained a central chamber, an early form of mausoleum, probably used by a single tribe or family around 5000 to 4000 BC.'

So infectious was his excitement that I set the nose of the little Ford at the one-in-four gradient and followed the sign.

The road was narrow, steep and high-sided, more in keeping with Devon than Herefordshire. Its route traced a twisting fold in the hill, while in contra-flow, a boisterous brooklet on the left side ran joyously downwards. Occasionally this lively stream, in its enthusiasm, spilled across the uneven tarmac to form a thin veil of moisture through which the little Ford splashed noisily.

Halfway up the hill, I passed a faded white-walled cottage, the windows full with yellowing geraniums and sad net curtains. An old man came bustling around the corner of the dwelling, his arms clutching a bundle of twigs for his fire. On seeing me he came to an abrupt halt and looked about nervously, like a frightened rabbit. Then he bolted through his front door and slammed it sharply behind him.

Further along, I encountered a small fenced paddock which, to my surprise, contained two dark brown donkeys with light beige muzzles, who peered at me comically from the remains of an old bus, or half a bus, a single decker that served as a stable. How odd, I thought, to find donkeys on the fringe of Wales, where one expected wild mountain ponies with windswept manes, galloping freely along the rocky shelves.

After a mile or so, the hedgerows and banks receded and the road became more exposed. A feeling of isolation and vulnerability crept into my soul as I arrived at the bleak summit of the hill. It felt a lonely place, a fitting prelude to my first sight of the ancient graveyard.

The road ran straight and true for another quarter of a mile and, as I rounded the next corner, I came upon it — 'Arthur's Stone' — or was it? Certainly it was ancient, with two great flat lichen-covered slabs weighing several tons a-piece, supported somewhat precariously by the stumpy weathered pillars beneath.

I skidded the little Ford to a halt on the uneven, gravelly surface; the engine died rapidly, as if thankful for the break, and I sat in silence, taking in the scene. For whilst the cairn may have been of great archeological interest to most, it was 'The Devil's Heap of Stones' to me, and I looked around hastily for the big black dog. Memories of my youthful Saturday mornings in Abergranog came flooding back as I thought of Aunty Dolly, her meat ration and the errand I used to run so regularly.

☆　☆　☆

Usually it was tenpence or a shilling, and if there was a square of corned beef or a little sausage, it came to about one and three.

It hardly made the big scales quiver. With sleight of hand, Mr Hodder the butcher would make it disappear into greaseproof paper and pop it inside the canvas frail. The ration book section would be scored out with a stubby pencil, the change from the two-shilling piece carefully wrapped and Aunty Dolly's meat for the week was on its way.

Saturday morning was always the same for me. I left on my errand at ten o'clock sharp, with the frail containing five small currant cakes that Mother had made, the ration book and the money.

'One lamb chop, not too fat. Go straight there and don't lose the change!'

Mr Hodder was the only butcher in Abergranog, advertising himself in big gold letters as a High Class Meat Purveyor.

His was a jolly shop, for he was always laughing and teasing the women as he eased his aproned bulk around the scrubbed blocks, chopping meat and sharing out the little extras.

It could take up to twenty minutes to get served, and I would pass the time making patterns in the sawdust on the floor or counting the cows, pigs and sheep painted on the tiled walls.

I seemed to spend every Saturday of my life collecting Aunty Dolly's meat, but it was worth it and not without its compensations.

Financially, it was worth sixpence a trip, plus five shillings at Christmas. Then there was the cup of tea and biscuits when I delivered, and I was allowed to play on the damp, out-of-tune, upright, mahogany piano in the middle room.

Aunty Dolly was an enigma, for she was not really my aunt. She was Mother's cousin, and although Mother made cakes for her and I collected the meat, she wasn't really liked by the rest of the family. I never quite understood why, but it was something to do with the time when Aunty Dolly's mother had kept the Castle public house. I once heard Mother say: 'Dolly thinks she's too good to work, always trying to be a lady on other people's money.'

But I didn't mind her and was used to her odd ways.

She was a small woman, crippled with arthritis, very forgetful, living as a recluse in a terraced house that always had the blinds drawn and stank of cats.

It was the same ritual every week. Between half-past ten and eleven I would arrive at Park View—rather pretentiously named, since it looked out over the remnants of a slag tip that, although sparsely grass-covered and sheep infested, was far from a rural scene.

The cast-iron gate was always half ajar, having been grounded in that position ever since its weight had pulled the hinges out of the brick pillar.

Five steep, moss-flaked steps led upwards to the narrow front door, obscured on one side by a faded sun curtain that remained half-drawn both winter and summer.

Rising to reach the knocker from the top of the steps always made me feel giddy, and I would back down quickly as my three customary bangs echoed through the passage beyond. Then there was the wait—about two minutes—the shuffling from inside, the mumbling and the sound of the cat.

I never knocked more than once because I knew she would hear, even though slightly deaf; she would in fact already be standing behind the door in anticipation of my arrival. This I discovered once when, before knocking, I took a brick from the wall and, standing on it, peered through the letter box, to spy the top of her thinning henna-red hair.

The door was swollen with damp and, when the latch was

released, she would start to drag it open. I had to wait for this, too. Once I tried to help by pushing from the outside; but she shouted, pushed it shut again and I had to wait longer.

When there was just about six inches of gap, an evil, slant-eyed head would slide around the bottom of the door and snarl. This was Megan, Aunty Dolly's ginger cat. I would have to put my boot in Megan's face to stop it coming out and the head would disappear.

It was funny about Megan, for at that time my veterinary knowledge was very limited and Wendel Weeks said all ginger cats were 'men' cats and told me how to tell, because his father bred champion wire-haired terriers and he knew.

But Megan didn't like me and scratched my face when I tried to do what Wendel advised—so much for one of my first clinical examinations.

'It's Hugh with the meat!' I would shout round the door. Only then would it open further, until it was wide enough for Aunty Dolly to look out.

Like a splattered tomato, red gloss lipstick covered the lower half of her puffy face, accentuating the ghostly white texture of her skin which was so heavily powdered that little clouds of dust filled the air when she moved her head.

With faded, watery eyes she would gaze right past me and only slowly return to focus upon my face. For earrings, brooches, bangles, beads and long fingernails, Aunty Dolly had no equal. Mother said she wasn't a lady, but I used to think she must have been, a long time ago.

When satisfied that it was indeed 'Hugh with the meat', she would leave her position behind the door; I had to squeeze round with the frail and then follow behind as she clattered down the passage in her brown and white high-heeled shoes and tight skirt, to make the tea.

She was a lonely soul but, despite the family antagonism, I liked her. She was always very concerned that I had enough tea and biscuits, never complained when I hammered on the piano and always came up with the money.

That's why I was so upset when the dog stole her meat.

It was my fault from the beginning. I had disobeyed orders. I didn't go straight there. I went the other way.

'Straight there' was left at the butcher's, past the police station, the Salvation Army, Oliver's Garage, down the Snatchwood Road as far as Biggs the Flowers, then up Park Pitch to Park Terrace and Park View.

The 'other way' was still left at the butcher's, but up the back of the police station, through the gulley by the British Restaurant, then round the side of the mountain—well, not really a mountain, but a big rising fold at the back of the village that eventually joined a ridge looking down on Abergranog.

On the skyline at the top of the ridge was a clump of boulders, not dissimilar to those now a few yards away—and they were called 'The Devil's Heap of Stones'.

I would go the 'other way' for one reason only: to gaze at this sight in awe, feeling the shivers up my back as I thought of the tales I had heard.

They said that if you went alone, sat on the biggest of the stones and made a wish, the Devil would grant it. But he would give you evil as well.

And he always did.

There was Nebo Prytherch who wished for a diamond ring and found one next to him on the stone. But the Devil told the police it belonged to Mrs Morgan the Bank and he went to jail.

Bronwen Pugh sat on the stone and a few months later had a baby. But the Devil told her dad some other tale and her dad threw her out.

Parky Brewer had wished for a new mower. He got one, and two weeks later it ran over his foot and cut off three of his toes.

I wanted long trousers and for some time had been

debating in my mind the risks I would be taking if I asked. That was the start of the trouble.

That fateful Saturday I had taken the 'other way' and was standing, mesmerised by the stones and thinking of my wish, when I thought I heard a voice say: 'If 'ew wants long-uns, Hugh bach, come on up an' they'm 'ewers.'

Putting down the frail, I advanced a few steps, hoping to hear it again. I stood. I leaned. I cocked an ear. Nothing.

Suddenly the silence was broken by a terrible growling at my back. My breathing stopped, my hair stood on end and my socks began to fall down. He was behind me.

My body was rigid and I spun round just in time to see a big black dog withdraw his head from the frail.

'Lay off, dog!' I shouted. But it was too late. He growled again, shook his head defiantly and sped off down the mountain with Aunty Dolly's meat in his mouth.

I covered my face with my hands, for it was hopeless to give chase. Whatever could I do? All gone. It was a week with no extras, not even a little sausage. I had money to buy another, but then there was the ration book—already the week's meat had been pencilled out.

Poor old Aunty Dolly, her chop for the week gone.

But it wasn't only my fault. I uncovered my eyes slowly and turned to face the stones.

'An' 'ewer's, too, 'ew mean Devil!' I said, as hatefully as I could. ''Ew never give me long-'uns. I never asked. But 'ew sent that dog to take the meat. 'Ew owes me!'

Tears of temper, full and burning, obscured my eyes. I grabbed the frail from the ground—the cakes and change still lying in the bottom—and, wiping my face, I marched up the hill to the stones.

Exhausted and full of anger, I eventually reached the flat one at the centre and sat down heavily. The morning dew still lay in patches on the surface and its crisp dampness met the back of my legs. The shock of the sensation ran through me and the realisation dawned of what I was doing.

No matter, I was determined to ask and looked upwards to the sky. Suddenly it struck me that I was appealing to the wrong department; I changed my line of vision, looking down the hill to the Boggy Pipe where the Avon Llwyd sneaked its way under the wood. There were rats and filth down there and I felt it would be more appropriate.

Taking a deep breath, I made my fatal request.

'Send us a lamb chop, Devil!' I demanded, with as much confidence as I could muster.

Three times I said it, crossing and uncrossing my fingers between each sentence. Altering the direction of my gaze, I looked down at the police station and tried again. I said it over and over, staring each time at places where I thought the Devil was most likely to be.

I waited and watched. Not a sausage, or even a piece of corned beef. It wasn't going to work.

"Ew'm a wash-out, Devil!' I cried. "Ew can't do it!'

Then I thought of all the excuses I could make—Hodder's was closed, or the ration book had a page missing, or I'd lost the money. But as I made my way down the mountain to Park View, I knew in my heart that I would have to tell Aunty Dolly the truth.

After she had dragged the door back, she didn't even notice that I had only said 'Hugh' and not 'Hugh with the meat', or the fact that I was later than normal.

Instead, she greeted me with a sort of smile that made the tomato paint explode, giving glimpses of her uneven, yellow teeth. I followed her up the passage and, when we got to the middle room where the piano was, she halted.

'Aunty Dolly,' I started to explain, 'the chop . . . ' But I never got any further, for my eyes saw the object on top of the piano.

Lying on a big round plate, with parsley sticking out of its bum and its legs tied with string, was a dead chicken—

ready to cook.

'Uncle Elwyn, from the country, came this morning,' Aunty Dolly croaked. 'Brought a chicken for Megan an' me.'

I breathed a sigh of relief. Saved. Saved by Uncle Elwyn's chicken. I could have kissed it. I realised that now was the time to come clean.

'The chop . . .'

'The chop,' she repeated, giving another clownish smile. 'Elwyn's chicken will be enough for us, boyo. 'Ew take the chop 'ome for 'ewer tea!'

She never saw the expression on my face, for the kettle started to whistle and she turned away.

'I've got a chocolate biscuit for 'ew. Special,' she was saying. That registered, for they were my favourite, and with one more thankful look at Uncle Elwyn's chicken, I followed her through to the kitchen.

All the way home I re-examined the situation. The Devil had really mucked it up this time. There was no way he could get back at me, because even if I had asked for a chop and he had tried to get Aunty Dolly to give me one, there wasn't one. I didn't have one. So we were quits.

And as for long trousers, summer was only just around the corner. They would be too hot then, anyway.

Happily, I ran up the alleyway by the side of our house. Mother was at the back door.

'You're late, Hugh. I was just beginning to worry.'

I gave no explanation.

'I've got a surprise for you,' she continued, with a twinkle in her eye. 'Guess!'

'Long-'uns,' I said at once.

'No—not long—'uns.' She appeared slightly bemused by the swiftness of my response. 'Uncle Elwyn has been up.'

'We've got a chicken!' I said, excitedly.

'No.' Her face set with puzzlement at my rapid guesses, for I was usually rather slow.

'Better than that . . .' She wiped her hands on her pinny and smiled at me. 'He's killed a lamb and brought us some lovely chops—I'm cooking one for your dinner.'

She disappeared into the kitchen and, as I stood there, a wonderful aroma wafted through the window. It was the Devil's Chop all right, and there were countless reasons why I shouldn't go anywhere near it. But as its fragrance filled the backyard, my nostrils began to quiver.

After all, I had asked for one . . . and besides, I was very, very hungry.

☆   ☆   ☆

How close is the past when one dreams. I got out of the little Ford and looked around for the black dog, but there was none, so I went up to the cairn and sat on the largest slab of stone.

What had previously appeared lonely and desolate now seemed peaceful and serene. To the west, the winter sunshine set in gold and silver glory, beaming low across the land. All that was white reflected its brightness, everything shiny glistened. Small cottages stood out importantly upon the hill and trees upon the ridge showed up in every twiggy detail.

Below me sheep, their woolly rumps towards the glow, grazed busily, completely unconcerned for the coldness of the night to come.

Already in the valley the wicked Welsh mist was gathering, poised to envelop as the sun turned its back and, in the hours of darkness when cold clawed at the mercury, to paralyse the Borders in treacherous, freezing fog.

But even though, if legend were true, I owed the Devil, there was such a thing as Devil's Luck. And as I looked around and thought of my life as a country vet, I reckoned that I had it.

6

Although a fair percentage of Herefordshire was populated by people of Welsh origin, Lasgarn was an uncommon name and I was often asked where I came from. Mrs Jarvis persisted in calling me Mr Lasgarnew, ever since my first visit when I had removed a fishbone from the mouth of Samson, her black cat, and had introduced myself as Lasgarn, Hugh.

Perhaps it was the interest in my own name that engendered my personal interest in others. If the geography and agricultural husbandry of Herefordshire was diverse, then the names of families, farms, villages and even fields, matched it in endless variety and were a continuing fascination to me.

The mixed fortunes of the Borders through the ages, having known Anglo-Saxon, Welsh and Norman influence, had left a mark not only on the architecture of the farmsteads, churches and Border castles, but also upon local terminology.

For instance, unlike other counties, there were many 'court' farms in Hereford. This made the dwellings sound rather grand and imposing—such places as Swanstone Court, Dormington Court, Elston Court and the like; or simply Court Farm, followed by the name of the hamlet or village, such as Court Farm, Mansel Lacy or Court Farm, Wormsley.

'Court' was a legacy of the Normans, from the French 'cours', which meant fold or cattle yard, usually enclosed and surrounded by walls or farm buildings. Indeed, in the practice there were still many farms where the farmer literally stepped out of his front door into the cattle yard, a feature no doubt dating from the time when stock were closely guarded against cattle thieves.

Topographical names were mainly derived from the Anglo-Saxons and included such terms for hills and dales as 'hope', 'croft', 'knoll', 'den' or 'lye'.

Place names often incorporated mediaeval terms as well. There was, for instance, 'ward'—a guarded place, as in Broadward; 'rich'—a kingdom, as in Goodrich; and 'batch' or 'bage'—a brook, as in Mowbage.

'Much' was used for great, as in Much Marcle, Much Birch and Much Dewchurch. Hampton was a common name, whilst others of a more peculiar character were Pennyplock; Scatterbrain; The Quob; The Stitches; Slatch, Turningways; Twizling and Chilson Orts.

There were many 'tumps', too, 'tump' being a peculiar term for a barrow hill; scattered throughout the area, they were the mounds of Early Norman strongholds. Surmounted by a palisade, a stone wall or even a tower, they served alike to keep down the conquered English and keep out the unconquered Welsh. The latter, when not playing home fixtures, were persistently harrassing the foreigners. There was Wormelow Tump, Cockyard Tump and Gallows Tump, and often the Tump, the Court Farm and the church were all found together.

Of the marauding Welsh there were few traces other than in the west of the county, where more lyrical place-names occurred, often having picturesque origins; like the isolated village of Clodock, nestling beneath the Black Mountain.

Clodock is a corruption of the Celtic name Clydag, a crowned prince, the son of Cledwyn, King of Ewias in the fifth century AD.

According to legend, Clydag eventually became King himself. One day he went out hunting with a man who, jealous of his relationship with a lady friend, killed Clydag.

On the day of the King's burial, the two oxen pulling his cart came to a ford across the river and, for some unknown reason, refused to cross. They caused such a commotion that the yoke joining them to the cart broke and, as a result, the dead King was buried near the bank of the river.

Such an act of murder made Clydag a martyr, and an enclosure was created around the tomb where his people would regularly gather to worship.

In time, a shelter of wood was raised and later, as there was plenty of stone in the area, a more permanent oblong building was erected. With the Norman Conquest, the building was further developed with a chancel, nave and tower, and so the resulting church, the village that grew round it and the parish are called Clodock, to this day.

No wonder the Black Mountain, towering above, had such a mystic air about it, with all it must have witnessed during its lifetime.

On the Welsh side, the populace were called Powell, Morgan, Lewis and Watkins and the farm names were often simply Welsh translations of their description: Brynhyfryd—the pleasant hill, or Cae-glas, the green field.

As for Herefordshire families, the Anglo-Saxons who had helped in the feuds had been designated clan names of distinction, ending in '-ing'. There was Billing, Holling, Tibbing and Monning, surviving as Ballinger, Hollings, Tibby and Manning.

Even closer to my heart lay the fascination in the names of the animals.

The Hereford Herd Book Society registered all the pedigree cattle and, accordingly, each had an individual number tattooed in its right ear.

The waxy surface of the inside of the ear flap was cleaned with spirit and the number 'set up' in the tattoo pincers, rather like newspaper type, except that the dyes were made of a metal base and the characters formed by sharpened

91

spikes. Tattoo paint or, on many occasions, blacklead, was pasted on the skin of the ear flap and the pincers applied with a sickening crunch. But when complete, the operation left an indelible and permanent identification imprinted in the tissue.

The number comprised the herd prefix, often the initials of the owner and the farm—for example, the Baynes at Wormcastle were BWC; to this was added a letter, depending upon the year—'M' for 1955, 'N' for 1956 and so on; this was followed, finally, by a serial number. A typical ear tattoo could be BWC/M16.

But as well as the number, there was also the name.

This would be prefixed by the Herd name, such as Eaton, Penatok, Sarn, Vern or Merryhill.

To avoid inbreeding new blood was often brought into the herd and, at that time, the Eaton Herd had, as senior stock bull, the magificent Vern Quantock; junior stock bull was the up and coming Donnington Prospero; there was a clutch of young bloods called Eaton Vanguard, Van Dyck, Vanderbilt and Victorious, all eager to make their name and feature high in the Hereford Herd Book.

The females, whose characters ranged from regal and noble to gentle and maternal, were the Countesses and Ladies; the Silks, Curlies and Oyster Maids.

There were famous sires like Penatok Norseman, Vern Rommel and Sarn Upsidedown and dams such as Princess Gem, Lowesmoor Regina and Hostess Cloudy.

So, with such a variety of place-names, family names and cattle names, conversation in the Borders was always colourful.

☆   ☆   ☆

It was when one came to the names of pets that difficulties arose in grasping the thinking behind them.

The pet or small animal work was steadily increasing

and, as a result, I decided to keep records of my patients' ailments and treatments on a card-index system.

Miss Billings originally scoffed at the idea, but when I told her that she would be in sole charge of the distribution, she developed more enthusiasm.

It was a simple system, recording date, breed, age, sex, ailment and treatment. Other information could also be written in, using an abbreviated form, such as APS—'a proper sod', or CB—'cheeky bitch', the remarks not always referring to the patient.

Amongst the dogs, there were of course Spots, Patches, Rexes and Chums, and the cats could be Ginger, Queenie or just plain Puss. But there were also Elvis, Marilyn, Softly, Stinky, Rinky, Betsy, Tiger, Jasmine and Mister J. (a very snooty pug).

But the one that will always remain in my memory was Monty, named after none other than Bernard Law Montgomery, First Viscount Alamein, the renowned Field Marshal whose energy, tenacity and fire routed the Germans from North Africa and sent them packing up through Europe.

The proud bearer of this illustrious abbreviation, named by his owner who had been one of the 'Desert Rats', was a tom cat, and a ginger one, at that!

He came on my first night in the new surgery premises. Bob Hacker had decided that the old greenhouse had served its time as a consulting room, and although the practice was predominantly agricultural, he realised that there was a considerable potential in the provision of a pet-care service which was much needed in the area.

I suppose that in the 'fifties we were just beginning to become aware of the hidden value of companion animals, whether they were smart pedigree types or nondescript but affectionate crossbreds. There was developing a realisation of their true place as part and parcel of our progressive, if somewhat confused, society.

So the exotic plant consulting room was demolished and in its place was erected a flat-roofed, brick extension.

Bob Hacker had a pal in Birmingham who had developed a thriving pet practice and it was from his premises that we copied the design for the interior.

The floor was of grey linoleum and the walls half-tiled in a light shade of green. There were long, low windows on three sides, complete with venetian blinds. In place of the old chest of drawers was a plastic-topped unit, above which was fixed a cupboard with sliding glass doors containing drugs on display. Instruments were accommodated in drawers in the unit below. A wash-hand basin with a geyser, for ever-ready hot water, was fitted in one corner and, for the centre, we had purchased a tubular-legged examination table with an easily cleanable and exceptionally smooth rubberised surface.

I remember questioning the fact that the top would be rather slippery for animals to stand upon; but Bob, who had researched the whole project extremely thoroughly, had a theory that if an animal felt insecure it was less likely to be aggressive.

A theory that was to be disproved on several occasions.

Although Monty came on the first night, he was fortunately the last patient.

Every one of the previous clients had been very complimentary about the new consulting room and had 'oohed' and 'aahed' at the fitments, from the adjustable examination light to the flip-top waste bin.

But when Monty arrived, his owner, Mr Sparks—he of the Desert Rats—thumped the roped-up orange box irreverently upon the smooth, sterile, brand-new surface of the examination table and announced:

'You're goin' to 'ave some bloody trouble with 'im!'

As he spoke, the orange box did a little jig across the smooth surface, leaving a jagged scratch from a loose nail

94

on its under-side.

I bent down and saw, between the thin wooden slats on which was imprinted 'Produce of Tangier', a pair of shining, green and distinctly evil eyes.

If the green eye of the Little Yellow God was fearsome, then this pair were even worse.

'You Mr Lasgarn?'

I nodded.

'You been highly recommended to me.'

His remark made me feel rather special, for it was the very first time I had been 'recommended', and no matter what the circumstances, to a recent graduate it was very satisfying.

Following this unexpected compliment, I listened with exaggerated interest as my client introduced himself and told me about his campaign in the Desert and the routing of the Hun—which took some considerable time—and how, in honour of the great leader of the campaign, every cat Mr Sparks had owned since had been christened 'Monty'.

On conclusion of the war epic, I placed my hand upon the orange box.

It was as if I had switched on an electric fan inside, for the action released a miniature tornado as Monty tested every rope and spar of his confinement which, considering it had only been constructed to transport sweet, ripe and completely inoffensive oranges, stood up to the onslaught extremely well.

When calm had resumed and both Monty and the orange box had come to rest, I enquired of Mr Sparks as to the purpose of the visit.

Mr Sparks screwed up his craggy features and massaged his chin with his exceptionally large hands, then said:

'I wants him neutralised!'

If names had their variety, their profusion was only exceeded by the different evasive phrases to describe the castration of the domestic tom-cat.

Ladies would often ask for them to be 'seen to', or 'attended to' or 'settled'. But there were other, more indelicate ways of putting it and although I had heard many, I was never surprised at the new descriptive terminology that came up.

'Neutralised' was yet another one.

'Gettin' a bit too much of a gentleman, if you take my meaning,' continued Mr Sparks. 'So we thought we'd ave 'im done. But you'll 'ave some trouble with 'im. I'll tell you that for nothin',' he added confidently.

The castration of the male had certain, indefinable moral connotation, for although bulls were castrated to make them less aggressive and fatten more readily as bullocks, stallions emasculated to render them more manageable and tom-cats 'neutralised' to make them less of a general nuisance—dogs were only rarely done.

McBean, of course, had the answer to that one: 'A dog, Hugh, is man's best friend—and there are some things you just wouldn't be doing to your best friend, would you, now?'

There was a small army of pig-killers in the rural areas, who often turned their hands—or their knives, to be more correct—to castrating. And as the Anaesthetics Act had not come into effect, speed and efficiency were supremely important in making the task humane.

However, when it came to tom-cats, we used the 'boot', a cat-length leather cylinder with ventilation holes at one end and two handles and a fold-over leather flap at the other.

The unfortunate victim was taken by the scruff and the hind legs and inserted into the 'boot', head first; the flap was then folded over and buttoned. Once in, the 'boot' was stood on end and held upright by the handles, securing the hind legs at the same time.

The operator, after disinfecting the appropriate area,

made two small incisions with a scalpel and smartly drew out the gonads, the whole procedure taking only seconds with a reasonable patient, who would often appear none the worse after the event.

Reasonable patient—that was the crux of it all.

And already I knew that Monty, like his indomitable namesake, had his own interpretation of what was reasonable.

I explained the procedure to Mr Sparks, who kept nodding his head as if he completely understood, but a wry smile on his face suggested that, beneath it all, he was a disbeliever.

Throughout the discourse, Monty had sat silently inside the orange box.

I prepared the swabs of disinfectant, cleansed the scissors needed to clip the fur; unwrapped the new blade and fitted it on to the scalpel handle; then took the 'boot' out from the drawer.

'If you hold this'—I demonstrated to Mr Sparks how I wanted it positioned—'I'll put him in.'

Mr Sparks nodded again, still registering his secret smile.

I tried not to appear nervous as I undid the ropes; animals could sense if you were nervous, so it was said.

But Monty still sat quietly.

When the last rope was unknotted and thrown back, however, he indicated his readiness with a low, threatening growl. It reminded me of the time, years ago, when I took a rabbit from Boggy, my first cat. I could see him now, green eyes flashing, as he wove towards me with just the tip of his tail flicking menacingly. At that moment, all loyalty and companionship between Boggy and me was abandoned— we were enemies. He would have reacted in the same way as Monty and I would have wanted him to, as well. Boggy would never have been 'neutralised' without a fight and, as I remembered my old pal, my respect for Monty grew.

I was no longer nervous, for it was fair game; whatever

fight the ginger tom in the orange box put up, he was well entitled to do so.

I decided to adopt his namesake's strategy of 'surprise being the essence of success in a military manoeuvre'—so I whipped off the lid and grabbed him by the scruff.

Monty went rigid, as if in spasm, his whole body quivering in the semblance of a fit. It was difficult to get a firm grip, for his posture rendered his skin taut and I could only hold with my fingers, rather than more firmly, with my palm.

'Ready, Mr Sparks?' I gasped.

He nodded, his features now devoid of any smile as he held out the 'boot'.

Right hand on Monty's neck, left over his hind-quarters, I lifted him out of the box, turning him in line with the 'boot'.

He didn't move. It was going too well.

With one eye on the open end of the 'boot', I drew the ginger tom back a few inches before thrusting him inside. Mr Spark's hand was shaking and I delayed my final move.

'You all right?' I asked.

It was this slight lapse of concentration that Monty had been waiting for. With a screech that would have frightened a werewolf, he coiled his body like a spring, so that my two hands were brought together, bringing his head in contact with my left hand and his hind legs with my right.

The synchronisation of his teeth and talons was perfect as they both dug into my flesh. With a yell, I dropped him onto the table, but his feet hardly touched the shining surface before he bounced, like a rubber ball, on to Mr Sparks' left shoulder.

'Steady, Monty,' I said, wringing my scarred hands.

Mr Sparks dropped the 'boot' and raised his arms towards his shoulder, but, like a flying squirrel, Monty soared five feet to land on the unit top, scattering swabs, scissors and scalpel.

A bowl of warm water and a pot of sulphonamide powder were the next to go, the white dust from the exploding canister enveloping Monty as he leaped from the unit top onto the roller towel. His weight pulled the holder from the wall and down he crashed.

But the fall did not in any way slow his momentum, for he did another three circuits of the consulting room before finally leaping onto the table, again to the unit top and, with one final bound, finishing up on top of the glass-fronted cupboard, well out of reach.

There he stayed.

'Told you 'e'd be trouble,' said Mr Sparks. 'Didn' I?'

There really was no answer to that, and Monty knew it. He just sat there, his green eyes glinting in the rays of the adjustable examination light, which had been swung round and was now upside-down, illuminating the ceiling.

'Come on, Monty,' I pleaded. 'Give us a chance.'

The ginger tom stood up and stretched, then raised his tail and, with a great flourish, waved it majestically, as if in salute.

That he turned round and piddled all down the front of the glass cabinet.

The smell was atrocious and there were gallons of it. He seemed to be going for ages.

There was a light broom in the corner, and as there was no other way to get at him, I decided to remove my rebellious patient from his lofty perch, using it as a persuader.

But the minute I picked it up, he was off again.

Two leaps and he was on the floor, one leap onto the window-sill, and then up behind the venetian blind.

The staccato clattering of the slats of the blind as Monty ascended from the far side was ear-splitting. Then, suddenly, there was silence and the blind, previously dancing like a frenzied concertina, became still.

I looked at Mr Sparks who had retreated to the far corner of the room.

The silence was uncanny.

' 'E's gorn!' said Mr Sparks.

And I knew that he was right.

In a flash I was outside; a glance at the wall showed the top section of the far window, which pushed out on a ratchet, hanging loosely, and all that remained of Monty was his aftershave — completely unforgettable.

Damn! The first care of any vet, when there is a cat in the surgery, is to make sure the windows are closed. Of course, with the posh new venetian blinds, the windows had been obscured and, anyway, who could have expected a cat to get up behind them?

'Sorry, Mr Sparks,' I said, back inside. 'It's my fault. We've lost him!'

'Oh, 'e'll come home,' he replied. ' 'E did the last time!'

'The last time?'

'When I took him to that other vet, Mr Brettner, down by the station.'

Mr Oswald Brettner and his assistant were the only other vets in Ledingford and, whilst relations between the practices were quite amicable, both kept their professional distance.

'Took him a couple of weeks ago for the same job,' continued Mr Sparks. 'That's 'ow I knew you'd 'ave trouble. Bit him through the finger as well and then got out through the fanlight.

'When he come home, I rang the vet, but he said to bring him here. Said you were more modern than 'im and were a specialist at this sort of thing. Yes, it was 'im that recommended you!'

Mr Sparks took his orange box and left.

I was standing, mulling over the recent events, my eyes smarting from the pungency of Monty's legacy, and thinking what a crafty devil old man Brettner was, when Bob Hacker popped his head around the door.

'Everything all right, Hugh?' he enquired cheerily. Then

he wrinkled his nose. 'Pooh! Tom-cats!' he exclaimed. 'Give you a tip, Hugh. Send that sort down to the opposition. If they're going to stink anywhere, better them than us, eh? Goodnight!'

I stood alone in the middle of the brand-new consulting room and surveyed the chaos—I still had a lot to learn!

☆ ☆ ☆

Fortunately, not all consultations in the new premises were as disastrous as Monty's, who, incidentally was allowed to keep 'his medals', as Mr Sparks put it later.

As well as dogs and cats, the clientele also consisted of cage birds and furry pets such as rabbits, guinea pigs and hamsters, who were mostly brought along by youngsters, sometimes accompanied by their parents and sometimes not. Yet it did not seem to matter, for when obtaining a case history, often the children knew far more about their pets than the adults, their powers of observation and memories being far more astute.

Sometimes, however, the truth took a little prising before it was revealed, like the day Colin and Tom Bell brought their golden hamster, Nosey.

Nosey was indeed a good name for him, for he was constantly investigating every nook and cranny of his surroundings.

Colin, being the elder, explained Nosey's problem, while little Tom stood back wide-eyed.

'He's got a swollen face,' he informed me. 'Just on one side, and he keeps scratching it with his claws.'

As if to confirm the symptoms, Nosey tapped his cheek vigorously with his paw.

'What have you been feeding him on?' I asked.

'Pellets, carrots, cabbage and grass, with water and sometimes milk to drink,' came the efficient reply.

'Nothing else?' I enquired, studying them both.

'No,' said Colin, looking perplexed that I should doubt his information, while Tom retained his stony silence.

Handling Nosey cautiously, for like all rodents, hamsters have powerful teeth and can bite viciously and gnaw their way easily through wooden structures, I felt the lump.

In hamsters there are two cheek pouches that the tiny creatures use to carry food to store behind their nests, but these are soft and on both sides. Nosey's lump was hard and confined to the right.

'I'll have to give your pet an injection before I can examine the inside of his mouth,' I explained. 'Come back at six o'clock this evening.'

I sedated Nosey with a minute dose of barbiturate and had completed my investigation by the time they returned and Nosey had revived from the anaesthetic.

'It's gone!' exclaimed Colin, as he peered into the box to see Nosey. 'The lump's gone!'

'Do you know what it was?' I asked.

For the first time, Tom spoke.

'Was it a sweet?' he asked nervously.

I unfolded the tissue on the table to reveal half a sticky humbug.

'Tom!' said Colin sternly. 'You gave Nosey that?'

Tom's eyes filled with tears.

'I thought it would be a treat for him,' he said.

I explained to them that too many sweets weren't good for small boys and positively dangerous for hamsters.

'They lodge in the cheek pouches and won't dissolve. Far better to give a piece of apple or pear for a treat,' I added. 'But don't worry, everything will be all right now.'

'An apple a day keeps the vet away!' quipped Colin brightly.

Tom forced a little smile and so did I, for, in Nosey's case, he was quite right.

Then there was the Jones family and Esther.

When you have a family of six, all under ten, and the pet is sick, it's a job to know who to leave behind when you visit the vet.

Mrs Jones had no problem—she brought the lot.

Two girls, four boys and the guinea pig.

'Sorry about this, Mr Lasgarn,' she apologised. 'But we all love Esther so much, that we all had to come.'

Meanwhile, Esther sat in the middle of the examination table, quite unconcerned that eight pairs of eyes at varying heights were gazing at her.

'Esther is losing weight,' Henry Jones, aged nine, informed me with a serious air. 'She has plenty of food and water, but she doesn't seem very hungry.'

'What do you feed her on?' I asked.

'Food from the pet shop,' said one.

'Carrots,' said another.

'Carrots and lettuce and bits of apple,' added a third.

'And hay,' completed Henry. 'But she leaves it all.'

I picked up the tiny creature gently, careful not to squeeze her chest and supporting her hindquarters with my free hand. She looked at me with sharp, intelligent eyes, her pointed features accentuated by her prominent incisor teeth. She gave a little squeak as I held her under the lamp.

'Your feeding is fine,' I said. 'But this young lady's most prominent feature seems to be the cause of the trouble. Her teeth are overgrown.'

My diminutive audience looked up at me, eyes wide and mouths open as I explained.

'You see,' I continued, 'guinea pigs' teeth are constantly growing, unlike ours, and unless they have something to wear upon, they become long and awkward. This makes it difficult for them to eat and that is why Esther is losing weight.'

'Will they have to come out?' asked Eileen, the fifth child.

I explained that that would not be necessary.

'Guinea pigs' teeth are not as sensitive as ours,' I told my

103

audience, 'and a quick snip with a dental clippers will do the trick.'

The rapt attention that followed as I trimmed Esther's teeth had to be witnessed to be believed.

'Will they grow again?' asked Cyril, the fourth.

'If Esther has something to gnaw upon, like a cabbage stump or even a block of wood, they will keep in shape. But check them every few weeks, just in case.'

'Could I have the bits of teeths?' asked Winnie, the youngest.

I was taken aback by the request, but scooped up the two small pieces of dentine and put them into her cupped hands.

'Of course,' I replied. 'But what are you going to do with them?'

Little Winnie Jones looked up at me with the face of an angel.

'When I lost my tooth, the fairies came in the night and gave me a sixpence. I thought Esther might get something, too.'

Children and their pets took special understanding, but the youngsters were often so trusting and caring that I enjoyed having them in the surgery. Adults and their pets, on the other hand, sometimes had difficulty in understanding *me*.

The classic example was Mr Flack.

When he first came to the surgery, he pointed to his hearing aid and then to Jack, his Cocker Spaniel, and I wondered if he was requesting a similar device for his pet.

It was always a bit tricky talking to Mr Flack, for despite his appliance, it still took four or five attempts to get the message over.

'Don't want him to get like me,' he squeaked in his high-pitched tone.

At this, Jack looked up with a rather insulted expression on his face.

'He heard that fine,' I commented.

'Yes. He's had it some time,' said Mr Flack, nodding his head.

'Ears?' I questioned.

'Not years, but certainly a few weeks,' he replied.

'His ears!' I tapped my own vigorously.

Mr Flack nodded in agreement.

The fact established, I commenced my examination of Jack's heavily matted, drooping ear flaps.

On lifting them, a rather objectionable odour hit my nostrils, the distinctive feature of inflammation of the outer ear, termed 'otitis'.

'Won't go like me?' enquired Mr Flack.

Had the conversation been easier, I could have explained that the inflammation was probably caused by bacteria and would not make Jack deaf. The fact that Spaniels had earholes covered completely by the flap allowed conditions to go unnoticed for long periods, often until the dog persistently shook its head, or the smell was obvious.

In the winter, especially, when dogs were lying closer to fires and radiators, the ears overheated and the inflammation was triggered off. Left untreated, the infection could affect the deeper regions of the middle ear, causing more severe symptoms. The dog could become quite ill and hold its head on one side, develop giddiness, lose balance and often walk in circles. Ear mites could sometimes contribute to the irritation, as could foreign bodies such as grass seeds.

However, I did not think that dear old Mr Flack would be that much better off if I attempted to tell him all that, so I gently passed my illuminated auroscope into the ear passage and through its magnifying lens was able to confirm my diagnosis.

'It's called otitis!' I said, clearly.

'Collar's too tight, is it?' Mr Flack looked puzzled.

'Inflammation in the ear!' I mouthed slowly.

After cleaning the ear passage, I inserted some ointment

and gave Jack an injection.

I held up the ointment tube.

'Put this in the ear,' I said, carefully. 'Every day.'

'Of course I'll pay!' snapped Mr Flack, taking out his purse.

Jack looked up at me and shook his head. It might have been the itch in his ears or it might have been an expression of his thoughts, for his eyes seemed to say: 'Silly old buffer!'

'Mind how you go,' I said, as I showed them through the door.

'You think it's going to snow?' asked Mr Flack, looking surprised.

'Silly old buffer,' I said to myself.

The following day, I got my little Ford stuck at Field Farm . . . in a snowdrift.

7

Whether my visit to Arthur's Stone had jogged the Devil's memory, or whether it was sheer coincidence, I shall never know, but just at the time when I was beginning to feel really at home in country practice, I got some evil—of a particularly disturbing nature.

It was a Wednesday evening, three weeks before Christmas. Bob Hacker, McBean and myself were in the surgery in St Mark's Square, discussing the purchase of some new equipment.

I had suggested a bone-pinning outfit, which enabled fractures of the long-bones of dogs and cats to be repaired without the use of Plaster of Paris. It was a fairly new technique, by which a stainless steel pin was inserted inside the shaft cavity of a leg bone, acting as an internal strut. When the fracture had healed, the pin was withdrawn through the orifice that had been drilled for its insertion. The method was far superior to plastering, for the odd shape of animal limbs, the weight of the cast and the reluctance of some patients to accept such cumbersome treatment, often made the success of the procedure less than perfect.

Bob was quite keen and, as we had already purchased a secondhand X-ray machine from the General Hospital, it would improve our small animal facilities considerably.

Our deliberations were interrupted by Miss Billings.

'It's Mr Matlin's cowman, from The Parks,' she announced. 'He's got a Milk Fever—she's just come in for milking and gone down in the stall.' She looked at Bob

Hacker enquiringly. Bob Hacker, in turn, looked at McBean—who looked at me.

I had no one to look at and the chain reaction terminated.

'I'll do it,' I volunteered, knowing full well that I had little option.

'Well, it's more or less on your way home,' said Bob.

'I'll get some hot water and warm the calcium,' added Miss Billings obligingly. And within minutes, I was on my way to The Parks.

The farm lay alongside the river, about two miles beyond Putsley, on the Woolford Road. The dairy herd was quite a large one; Mr Matlin, who owned it, milked about fifty pedigree Friesians, with the help of his cowman.

It was drizzling as I left the lights of Ledingford and drove east to my case. I did not waste any time and was soon splashing up the puddled lane, to turn off at the buildings in the direction of the milking parlour. But before I had halted, Mr Matlin's cowman, Chris, appeared at the door and waved his hands in a cross-over fashion, at waist level.

By the time I had stopped and wound down the window, he was across the yard, peering in on me, and the significance of his actions became clear.

'Too late. She's dead!' he panted. 'I was just going across to the house to stop you coming.'

'Sorry about that,' I said, perturbed at the unexpected calamity. 'I got here as quick as I could.'

'Oh, not your fault,' said Chris, recovering his breath. 'She looked a bit wobbly when she came in, and in minutes she just flopped on the floor. By the time I'd rung you and come back, she was gone. Probably a heart attack. Boss is away as well. Just my flippin' luck to lose a cow when he's not here.'

'When's he coming back?' I asked.

'Saturday,' he said. 'Gone up to Smithfield for the week.'

'I'll do a *post-mortem* if you like,' I suggested. 'Probably best, in the circumstances. Where are you sending her?'

'Alf Baldwin's. That's where they usually go.'

'Don't expect he'll fetch her tonight,' I said. 'But give him a ring, anyway, and I'll pop down to his yard in the morning.'

'Sorry you had a wasted journey,' said Chris.

'Win some, lose some,' I replied—and with that, turned in the yard and set off back to my digs.

The following morning, when I appeared for breakfast, Brad commented on how smart I looked, my improved appearance being mainly attributable to the fact that I was wearing a new sports jacket.

Diana had been cajoling me for some time into buying one and, after much resistance, for I was never a great one for shopping, I finally succumbed and purchased a green tweed Harry Hall at Benning's, one of Ledingford's best county outfitters. It had cost me a fair part of a month's salary, so I was pleased to have Brad's approval.

'I've got a free afternoon, so I'm meeting Diana for lunch,' I told her. 'Thought I'd give her a surprise.'

I had nothing booked for the morning and, as McBean was doing early surgery, I decided to call at Alf Baldwin's yard on my way.

His place was near the sewage works on the outskirts of Ledingford, a desolate area, populated mainly by rats and seagulls. I had heard from McBean that one could get excellent tomato plants for nothing, from the chap in charge of the filter beds, but they didn't appeal to me at all.

Alf's place was a square stockade of black, corrugated tin sheets, a quarter of which was roofed. At the side, two doors opened outwards, allowing his high-sided wagon to off-load the carcases he collected from the farms in the vicinity.

Normally the doors were open and Alf and his assistant, Stan, could be seen busily stripping and gutting. The stench was horrid, but having been so long at their grisly trade, their sense of smell had become dulled and unresponsive. Their characters, too, seemed withdrawn and they worked steadily and silently amid the gore, without undue comment or concern.

Many was the time I had been down to the yard when, even after the normal social courtesies of 'Good morning' or 'Good afternoon', I would have to wait several minutes before Alf finished the job in hand. Only then, after inspecting his knife for notches, or wiping his nose with the back of his hand, would he respond. Once, I had to follow several *post-mortem* examinations, and had visited the yard on at least five consecutive days and jokingly asked: 'Do you do Bed and Breakfast here?'

Alf continued to carve away at the neck of an old sheep carcase; when he had finished, he held up the meat, looked at me with just half a smile on his sallow, wrinkled face and said:

'No, Mr Lasgarn. Only evening meals.'

That Thursday morning, however, all was silent at Alf's yard, save for the squealing of the seagulls and the chattering of the engine in the sewage shed.

The tin doors were closed. A chain and a large padlock linked the posts through a square hand-hole in the tin, by which the bolt, on the inside, could be drawn.

I got out and peered through the hole, into the yard. The floor was wet and appeared to have been freshly hosed. I could see a pile of hides in the corner, the insides covered with saltpetre; the top one, although the hair was underneath, was black and white, like a Friesian cow.

If it was the one from The Parks, either Alf had made a very early start, or he had collected the cow on the previous night. I didn't know her tag number, so I could not check, but I was aware that Alf kept a work book in the boarded off section, that he grandly called the 'Office', and it would probably be in there.

Then I noticed that, although the lock was large and

seemingly invulnerable, it was also rusty and seized-up, acting as nothing more than a hook to link the chain. I undid the fastening and pulled open the tin doors. They clattered and rattled, provoking a scrabbling and a scurrying from inside, and, as I entered, I just caught sight of the tail-end of a party of grey rats, disappearing beneath the tins.

There was a freshly stripped rib cage of a cow, together with other assorted bones in a pile, and a set of cow's entrails nearby. Inside the covered portion were some cuts of meat, hanging like washing on a line. I had to dodge between them to get to the 'Office' door, which was swollen and juddered when I opened it, springing back finally with such force that it nearly threw me off balance.

Inside the small enclosure was a Pickwickian-type desk, tall and inkstained, with a tattered high stool as its motley companion. On the lid, resting amongst a jumble of pencils, ear tags, knives, sharpening stones and Woodbine packets, was the work book—a 1947 diary advertising a London insurance company. And there, in the column for Easter Sunday, was the entry: 'Matlin, The Parks. One Freeshun Cow', scrawled in thick, black pencil, with a tick alongside.

Must be the one, I thought. Damn! Already cut up. The situation made any reasonable diagnosis somewhat difficult.

It was hardly worth going back to the car to get my boots and apron in view of that, so I just picked my way over the yard, to take a cursory glance at the pile of guts.

I identified the stomach and intestines; the liver looked rather blue and the only visible kidney showed a considerable amount of haemorrhage on its capsule. But lying to one side, about four times its normal size, was the spleen—and when I saw it, a cold shiver ran down my spine.

I stooped down, just to make sure my eyes weren't deceiving me, and as I did, my pathology notes flicked rapidly, page by page, through my mind.

'Tumour of the Spleen—Infection of the Spleen—Congestion of the Spleen—all possible. But beware!' I could feel the eyes of the Bomber, Professor Bardsley of the Pathology Department at Glasgow University, burning down upon me from the heavens. 'Petechiated enlargment of the Spleen . . .ANTHRAX!'

I stood up and widened my field of vision, taking in the whole scene. It couldn't be Anthrax, surely—it was a Milk Fever. But I only had Chris's word for that, and he wasn't a vet. I hadn't seen the cow, but then, I had had no need to see it. Indeed, if I hadn't been so prompt, he would have telephoned to stop me going.

But these arguments didn't solve the immediate problem. Was it or wasn't it?

I had never seen an Anthrax case before—not many vets had—but in the depths of my mind I was feeling distinctly uneasy.

Take a swab . . . check it out.

Back to the car I went and rummaged through the kit. I could sense panic creeping over me as I found the swabs and glass slides.

I took a touch smear of the blood and pushed the cotton wool swab deep into the black pulp of the grossly enlarged spleen. And as I drove to the surgery, I shuddered to think of the possible consequences.

Anthrax is caused by an organism that kills by invasion. Most animals, including man, are susceptible and, because it multiplies into millions within hours of infection, it is highly contagious.

That was why it was termed a Notifiable Disease, similar to Swine Fever, Rabies and Foot and Mouth. Any suspected case of Anthrax had to be reported to the police, who then informed the Ministry of Agriculture, who took control of the disposal of the carcase and subsequent disinfection of the premises.

Because the germs produced extremely resistant spores

when exposed to air, the carcase, unopened, was burned on the spot, or as near to the spot as practicable, under police supervision. There were even provisions for the correct proportions of the funeral pyre, with regard to the amount of wood, coal and inflammable material necessary and the dimensions of the plot. And the local constabulary had to remain in attendance at the bonfire until all the remains had been completely cremated.

In Herefordshire, the commonest cause of spread was through 'shoddy' or bonemeal, two commodities used in the hop yards.

'Shoddy' was the woollen waste from the milling factories in the North, which remained after imported fleeces had been sorted. It was packed around the young hop bines to act as a fertiliser. But often, Anthrax spores contaminated the imported product, even infecting humans at the mills, where it was known as 'Wool Sorter's Disease'.

The disease in humans caused skin rashes in its mildest form and death in its most acute.

Bonemeal, if imported and unsterilised, was another source of infection and was, again, used extensively in hop farming.

Sudden death in a beast on a hop farm was therefore always treated with suspicion. A blood smear was taken after making a minute incision in the ear vein of the dead animal, and stained for evidence of the disease, before the carcase was even moved. Until this had been done, opening the carcase was against the law.

And mine had not only been moved, but was in bits—all over the yard!

'Good morning, Hugh,' smiled Miss Billings as I burst into the surgery. 'My, don't you look smart. By the way, Mrs Pegler wants you to ring about Bertie. She's been awake all night worrying about him.'

At that particular moment, I had unkind thoughts about

113

Mrs Pegler and her precious Bertie and barely grunted an incoherent reply. Miss Billings responded with a look of surprise rather than reproof, for even first thing in the morning I was normally quite amiable.

I charged down the cellar steps, two at a time, to the small laboratory where we kept the microscope, stains and other equipment for analysing samples.

The first step was to fix the blood smear on the slide, by passing it through a flame. I connected the Bunsen Burner to the gas tap and looked for the matches . . . none!

Back up the steps, three at a time.

'MATCHES!' I shouted at Miss Billings.

She looked aghast. 'Matches?'

'I've got a slide for Anthrax and there's no matches!'

'Oh!,' she gasped. 'Oh dear!' She searched through the desk drawer. 'There aren't any, you'll have to go next door!'

Outside I chased, the door bell clanging hysterically behind me, and into Griffiths' the Grocer, next door. It seemed to take an age until I got to the counter and purchased the matches.

I was making for the door when Mrs Griffiths called: 'Mr Lasgarn!'

Oh, God! I thought, if she was going to ask about her cat, I would just have to be rude. Perhaps it was the change. I opened my palm to check and found it correct, so I turned back to the counter.

'Nasty stain on your jacket,' she said. 'What a pity—such nice material, too.' I must have looked puzzled. 'On the shoulder,' she continued.

I passed my hand over my back. There was a damp patch, and when I looked at my fingers, they were red.

It was blood, from the meat at Alf Baldwin's.

Back in the cellar, I flamed the slide, then added the methylene blue for a minute. Carefully rinsing the excess stain away, I dried out my specimen and placed it on the stage of the microscope.

114

My hands were shaking so much, it took me several attempts to focus.

Finally, I turned the fine adjustment knob, the blue mass became more distinct and, as the lens distance narrowed, I could pick out the myriad, tiny circles of the blood corpuscles with, occasionally, a larger cell lying between.

But as I gingerly moved the slide sideways, they came into view . . . small, rectangular, round-ended chains, surrounded by pink capsules — *railway trucks* — the distinctive and unmistakable description of *Bacillus anthracis* — ANTHRAX.

I had got a case of the dreaded disease, literally on my hands.

I fetched McBean.

'Mother Mary and all the Saints!' he exploded. 'Where the hell did'ye get this?'

'Matlin, The Parks,' I said, and told him all that had happened.

When I had finished my story, he stood, leaning heavily against the lab table, the Bunsen still roaring away behind, and fixed me with a questioning glare, more in incredulity than disbelief.

'We must inform the Ministry, and of course the police,' he said, finally.

'There's something else,' I added. McBean's hands tightened. 'I've got blood on my jacket.' I turned sideways to show him. 'I got involved before I realised and must have rubbed against the meat when I opened the office door. There were a few pieces hanging up.'

'A few pieces!' exclaimed McBean. 'There should have been a whole cow!'

My mind instantly ran back to Alf's 'washing line'. There was a fair bit hanging up, but in no way a whole carcase.

I pictured the yard again — hides, bones, offal, but no more meat.

'It wasn't all there,' I said. 'A lot of it was missing!'

115

McBean went white. His hands blanched as he gripped the table top.

'Mother Mary! Don't say he's sold it!' He put his hands to his face, as if protecting himself from a sudden and unexpected bright light. For some time, he stood as if struck. Then he jerked back into life, dropped his hands and shouted:

'We've got to get Alf, before we ring anybody!' He pushed past me. 'What's his number?'

'I don't know,' I replied rather lamely.

'I'll get it!' he shouted again. 'And get that bloody jacket off and put it in a bag!'

'What about my shoes?' I asked.

'Those as well!' he rasped. 'Hugh! For all I know, you could be a bloody walking plague!' And with that, he dashed away up the steps.

Lunch with Diana was going to be late.

What followed may, in retrospect, make interesting and even, perhaps, humorous reading, but for me it was one of the most distressing occasions of my early veterinary life. For even though it lasted, initially, only a few hours, I worried for weeks about the possible consequences.

Alf Baldwin had gone to the Midlands, where his brother-in-law sold pet food. Alf had been asked to supply some meat rather urgently and, thinking that the offal would be sufficient for me to make a diagnosis, had left earlier that morning.

The Ministry went into a flat panic when they heard. The police set up road blocks and Alf and his wagon were eventually stopped on the outskirts of Wolverhampton and had a police escort to his brother-in-law's yard, where the Ministry promptly slapped a Form A on him, temporarily closing down his business.

Alf's wagon was impounded, as were all his clothes, so he had to borrow a suit and come home on the train.

But instead of being justifiably annoyed and crying out for compensation, as he might have done, Alf was tickled pink by the whole affair.

'There I was,' he said, his sallow old features wreathed in smiles. 'There I was. Police car in front, two motor bikes be'ind, lights aflashin', going through the centre of Wolverhampton like the clappers. Who'd 'ave thought it, Alf Baldwin an' his knacker wagon, just like Royalty!'

As for me, I had a course of penicillin injections at the General Hospital, as a precaution, from the same doctor who had stitched me up a few weeks previously.

'Aiming for an early retirement?' he asked jokingly. But I didn't think it funny. And to add to that, they took my clothes as well and incinerated them: my shoes, my trousers, my shirt, socks and tie—and, above all, my new Harry Hall jacket.

The following Wednesday I was up before the Ministry, who had instigated an enquiry.

The Divisional Veterinary Officer, the Regional Veterinary Officer and, whilst not God Himself but fairly close, an Assistant Chief Veterinary Officer, an ACVO, all came to interview me. Three Scots, like kirk elders, dark suited and bespectacled, they sat at one end of a large table in the local Ministry office, while I sat alone, at the other.

It was like the Caine Mutiny—and, boy, did they give me a grilling.

The ACVO led the interrogation.

'Why did ye allow the carcase to be moved, laddie?'

'I saw no reason why I shouldn't.'

'Did ye no suspect Anthrax?'

'No. I thought it was Milk Fever.'

'How did ye know, if ye did'na check the beast?'

'I took the cowman's word for it. I had no reason to disbelieve him. Had it been a hop farm, I would have been more suspicious.'

With that, the Assistant Chief Veterinary Officer leaped up and thumped the table with his fist, startling both me and his two colleagues.

'It was, laddie!' he shouted. 'It was!'

I didn't understand. The Parks was a dairy farm—there were no hops.

'They were 'aw grubbed up, five year ago,' continued the ACVO. 'But the spores, laddie, the highly virulent spores of *Bacillus anthracis*, were still hiding secretly in the soil, waiting for their freedom. Then what happened?' He looked accusingly down the table at me. 'Along came the River Board and ditched the meadow to alleviate the floods, but they opened the door, laddie, and awa' the germs went!'

He then embarked upon a thirty-minute sermon, as much, I suspected, for the benefit of his colleagues as for me, but there was no doubt that he knew his stuff.

Commencing with Dr Robert Koch's famous paper of 1876 on Anthrax, he described the family tree of the anthracoid bacilli in copious detail: their potency, resistance and method of invasion; the pathology, diagnosis and principle of control. Then, as a judge before reading sentence, he quoted word for word, in Burnsian manner, the Anthrax Order 1938 and the Diseases of Animals Act 1950.

The only ray of hope to be gleaned from his whole oration was that, due to the cold weather, sporulation and the activity of the organism would be minimal and, as the carcase had all been located and destroyed within twenty-four hours, the risk of contamination was small.

'But,' added the ACVO, 'if this had been North Africa—it would have been a catastrophe!'

Eventually I was dismissed by the Three Wise Men and informed that my error had been noted and that, from then on, the Ministry would be ever watchful of my progress.

'Go Forth and Sin No More!'

As I walked down the hallway a girl passed me, bearing a tray with cups and a teapot.

'Aren't you stopping for tea, Mr Lasgarn?' she asked.

And I just about managed to say: 'No, thank you.'

That night we went to a dance; Diana thought it would cheer me up. The group were becoming very popular—Kenny Ball and his Jazzmen, at the Merchants' Hall.

McBean came, too, with his girlfriend, Mimi Lafont. He was very kind, bought a lot of whisky and said that if he had gone to The Parks, it would have happened to him instead—but I couldn't believe that.

I suppose I was a bit of a misery that night and was glad to get home to bed.

As I lay there, the strains of Kenny Ball's trumpet going through my mind, I could hear the sound of the railway trucks being shunted in the Farrs Court Sidings.

Railway trucks, that was a joke.

There had been a goods siding in Abergranog and, on a still night, you could hear them clanging and banging, too. I used to listen to them when I was a boy.

I lay awake, thinking of those early days. The days of the War, and the trucks, and the Metal Train.

And Albert Portman.

Albert Portman and the Ink-Drinkers.

☆   ☆   ☆

When Mr Pugh, Class Four, blew 'Lines' with his whistle on a string, the blast paralysed the whole playground.

'All boys stop dead and put hands by sides,' was the order demanded by the signal.

And everybody did . . . except Albert Portman.

Whilst the rest of us stood immobile, rigid to attention in whichever direction we were facing when playtime was brought to a halt, Albert Portman would round his shoulders, let his arms swing loosely in front of him, bow his legs, jut out his jaw and jump up and down like a monkey.

Wherever you were in the playground, it was impossible not to be aware of Albert's act, for if he was behind and out of sight he could still be heard going 'Ooow! Ooow! Ooow! Ooow!' just like a monkey.

You would have thought the boys would burst their shirts laughing or Mr Pugh go red-wild, like he did in Class Four when there was talking.

But no.

No boys sniggered or looked round, and Mr Pugh never showed any reaction other than to jingle the money in his pocket with his right hand, which he did often, and then blow a second shrill blast on his whistle.

At the second blast, everybody moved.

When the 'Lines' had been formed and settled, Albert would lope along from his spot in the playground, just like a monkey. Then, after moving up and down the lines, cocking his head on one side now and again to go 'Ooow! Ooow! Ooow!' to some boys standing to attention, he would come down to our class, Class Two, Miss Webb's, and stand behind Freddie Richards and in front of me.

Still jerking gently up and down, but with slightly softer 'ooow — ooows', he would wait with the rest of us until the third whistle.

'All boys move off in orderly fashion to class, starting with Class One, with no running, talking or spitting on the tiles while going upstairs.'

Once within the school building, Albert regained his normality and would maintain his pace within the straggling grey crocodile that wound its way from the freedom of the playground to the bottom-aching seats of learning, behind the twin desks at Abergranog Council School.

Albert's 'monkey act' started on the very first day he came to 'Big School' from the 'Infants'.

On that day, when 'Lines' were blown, the boys did snigger and Mr Pugh stopped his money jingling, and did go red-wild. He stormed up to Albert, grabbed him by his woolly jersey and dragged him into 'Lines'.

On the second day, when Albert repeated his performance, Mr Pugh cuffed his head and again pulled him into order.

But on the third day it was too much even for Mr Pugh. Popping with rage, the old gent left the playground with us all standing 'hands by sides', rattled off up the stairs and came back within minutes, with Mr Tom Davies, Headmaster.

Mr Tom Davies, Headmaster, was a gentle sort of man. He walked slowly up to Albert, who was gyrating like a drunken top and 'ooow—ooow-ing' as fast as he could, and stood for some time watching him.

'Albert,' said Mr Tom Davies, as the little hunched-up figure danced up and down on the spot. 'Albert, you mustn't do this when "Lines" are blown. You must stand still like all the other boys, then run to your line at second whistle.'

But Albert was oblivious to the request and just kept 'ooow-ing' and jumping up and down, like a monkey.

'Blow second whistle, Mr Pugh,' said Mr Tom Davies, Headmaster. 'I'll see to Albert.'

Second whistle was blown and, amid giggles and low whispers, 'Lines' were formed, rather irregularly, for most heads were half-turned to see what fate befell poor Albert.

To everyone's annoyance, third whistle was blown almost immediately, with the order to lead off to class.

The last glimpse I had of Albert and Mr Tom Davies, Headmaster, was as I passed between the pillars at the bottom of the stairs. Albert was still monkeying up and down and Mr Tom Davies, hands on hips, was standing silently, watching him.

We all thought Albert was in for a terrible time and, as he didn't come back to class that afternoon, we decided he had received a severe strapping and been sent home.

But he didn't come back the following day.

Or the next day, either.

Or the day after that.

And even after the weekend, he didn't come back on the Monday.

The rest of the family did nothing to relieve our gnawing curiosity.

There were five Portmans in school, or four without Albert. There was Bendy in Class One, Albert in ours, Class Two; Victoria in Class Three; Baggy in Class Four and Kaiser Portman in Class Five. Bendy and Baggy were nicknames, Bendy due to the shape of his legs and Baggy due to his ill-fitting trousers, but Albert, Victoria and Kaiser were real.

We missed Albert in Class Two, for he was exceptionally good at sums and could answer multiplication long before the rest of us, even thirteen and above.

He could draw, too. He drew the most beautiful pictures of trees and ponds and mountains; but always, somewhere in the picture, was a little monkey. Not very big, but it was a monkey all right. You could tell by its face and its tail, and it was always smiling.

When Miss Webb asked what it was, he would say shyly: 'A cow, Miss,' or 'A cat, Miss,' or 'A dog, Miss,' or 'A sheep.'

But never a monkey.

Miss Webb would look over her glasses and say: 'But Albert, it looks like a monkey.'

But Albert would have none of it; he would shake his head in vigorous denial and go silent.

About two weeks later, when Miss Webb was teaching us about how the Earth goes round the sun and how, in the Ice Age, the big glacier had come down the valley, past Delly Evans' farm, round by the Big Cutty, down Cwm Road and out through the station—Mr Tom Davies, Headmaster, came into class.

We were all supposed to stand up when Mr Tom Davies
came in, but as we were about to put down our pens and lift
up the wooden seats, he waved his hand and said:

'Sit down, class. I just want to have a word with Miss
Webb.'

They chatted in low, serious tones for some time. Miss
Webb always seemed to be in a dream when Mr Tom Davies
spoke to her and said 'Yes, Headmaster. Oh. Yes, Headmaster', to every few words he said.

At last, he straightened up from the stooping position he
had held over Miss Webb, smiled at us all and left.

When the door had banged shut, Miss Webb woke up
and faced us.

'Now, Class Two,' she said, in her usual, singy voice, 'I
want you all to listen carefully to what I'm going to say.'

She ran her eyes up and down to make sure we were
attending.

'Some time ago, we had a little boy in class who thought
he was a monkey.'

'Albert Portman, Miss!' shouted Boxy Potter.

'That's right, John,' she observed, as Boxy puffed out his
chest, 'but please don't interrupt me again.'

Boxy wrinkled his nose with a sulk. He was always
answering right and puffing out his chest, and was none
too popular with the rest of us.

'As you all know,' Miss Webb continued, 'Albert has
been away for some time. He has been away having special
lessons. On Monday he is coming back to School and is
going to have lessons with us again.'

Several bottoms shuffled on the wooden seats at the news
and I saw Boxy make his mouth go like a monkey, but no
sound came out. Miss Webb missed Boxy's silent comment
and folded her arms on top of her desk.

'Now, Albert is a clever little boy, as you know, very good
at his tables and sums, but just at the moment he is having

a little trouble with a monkey.' She leaned forward in the same way that Mr Tom Davies, Headmaster, had done when he was talking to her and said slowly and clearly:

'So that Albert will not be upset, we are not going to take any notice if at any time he pretends he is a monkey, or if he draws a monkey, or if he makes a noise like a monkey. We just pretend he is saying something normal, and we will not laugh or giggle.' Miss Webb surveyed our somewhat bemused faces, adding sweetly, 'I know you will all help Albert.'

Then she put on her bossy voice and, directing her gaze to our corner, said firmly, 'Anyone not helping will get the Strap!'

So that was why Albert was allowed to continue his antics, and soon everyone was so used to them that it would have been unnatural if he had been stopped. He seemed no worse and no better than before, doing occasional monkey tricks in class, and regular ones in 'Lines'.

He was put at a double desk near Miss Webb, with Cedric Bowen, who was one of the 'Ink-Drinkers'.

There were three 'Ink-Drinkers' altogether: Cedric, who started it and Wilf and Ivor who copied him.

Cedric was a cousin to Wilf and Ivor, who were brothers. The three were compulsive ink-drinkers and drank from the little china pots in the slots on the desk tops. It was always easy to tell when they had 'been at the ink', for their blue lips and tongues gave them the appearance of terminal heart cases. Because of their addiction, they were made to sit in the front and use pencils rather than the red, wooden-handled pens that everyone else wrote with.

Albert and the Ink-Drinkers formed a little gang and kept very much to themselves.

At playtime they always spent the break sorting through the War Effort Pile, which was situated in a recess behind the lavatories. This odd collection of redundant metal accumulated from the scrap that everyone was encouraged to bring to school, to build bombs and tanks for the troops.

The metals were to be melted down to fashion the articles of war, a fact that had little impact on our sensitivities in Abergranog at the time. The rigours of austerity were nothing new, and it was left to the LDV, with their armbands and wooden sticks, to remind us of the slaughter that was taking place elsewhere in Europe. The LDV or Local Defence Volunteers constituted the 'last ditch' defence force for each locality and was manned by all those who, for reasons of age or other form of exemption, were unable to enlist. Led by a 70-year-old retired Sergeant Major, they made up in spirit what they may have lacked in impetus. This ragged band later became the Home Guard, but until that time, when they were more adequately kitted and armoured, their uniform was but an armband and their weapons as rudimentary as those of their mediaeval forebears.

What passed as scrap in those days could well have fetched a small fortune at a later date, in the up-market antique shops, but the brass bedsteads, pewter teapots, candlesticks, copper kettles and old keys all went into the melting pot.

Albert and the Ink-Drinkers were always sorting through the pile of metal. Occasionally one of them would find something interesting, and his pals would gather round, with Albert 'ooow-ooow-ing' with excitement. They never stole anything from the collection, for at the time it was all rubbish. They just seemed to get a great deal of pleasure ferreting through it.

Sometimes they put nuts and bolts inside teapots and shook them, like the Salvation Army. They would make a terrible racket, while Albert jumped up and down like a dervish.

They found a metal washboard and rubbed it up and down with a stick; Cedric Bowen took to banging saucepan lids together; and the day they found the trumpet they nearly went hysterical.

It was a pretty battered instrument and only partly functional, as the taps were half-closed. Sometimes it made trumpet sounds, but mostly rude noises like the Co-op horses, as they pulled the carts up Bowen's Pitch.

To see Albert Portman and the Ink-Drinkers parading about the playground, Albert leading with the trumpet, Wilf with the washboard, Cedric with the lids and Ivor bringing up the rear rattling a teapot, was a sight and sound to remember, especially when the Bowens were blue with ink, for they were still getting it from somewhere.

When the whistle blew for 'Lines', they carefully hid their instruments in the pile, ready to continue the performance at the earliest available opportunity. Albert was always last coming from the pile, secreting his battered trumpet within the metallic depths before running straight to his line.

There was no monkeying any more.

The little band practised every playtime and the crude cacophony gradually became acceptable to our ears, so that at times boys could be seen clapping their hands, or doing little jigs as the troupe wound in and out of the scattered gatherings on the yard.

It must have been summertime, because I remember the lavatories were smellier than usual. I had badly wanted to 'go' and, at the bell, had run straight out of class and made swiftly for the 'Boys'.

Shivering with relief, I was standing in the doorway when Albert and his little gang arrived.

They passed me without a word and disappeared into the recess.

I heard the high-pitched shriek, despite the rush of water that happened to leave the cistern at the same time.

It wasn't a human cry; it was so clear and earsplitting, so terrible, as if it was the final expression of tumultuous anguish.

Stepping out of the lavatory doorway, I leaned warily round the corner and looked into the recess. The Bowens stood in a forlorn little trio and, in front of them, on his knees, sobbing so that his whole body shook, was Albert.

The War Effort Pile had gone.

'Bob Brewis's lorry took it all last night, after school.' It was Boxy Potter, right again, who had pushed himself to the front of the rapidly assembling crowd of spectators. 'Took it all down to the goods siding and loaded it on the trucks. Goin' to Cardiff today it is, on the Metal Train. My brother's firin' the engine.' He puffed out his chest at the family connection.

Albert had ceased sobbing and sat huddled and still.

'All be melted down,' continued Boxy, glorying in the fact that he knew more than the rest of us. 'Guns an' bombs an' tanks to kill the Germans!'

At Boxy's last remark, Albert leaped up and spun round, his face tight and pale, eyes still awash with tears.

He made two 'ooow-ooow-s', then charged at the group of onlookers, flailing his arms as he went. The boys parted ranks at the onslaught and we all stood, speechless, as Albert ran full pelt across the yard, out through the big green iron gates, across the road and down into the Dingle.

When Mr Pugh blew 'Lines', Boxy told him what had happened, and when we went upstairs I saw Mr Pugh knocking on the door of Mr Tom Davies, Headmaster.

Next morning, Mr Tom Davies, Headmaster, had us all to stand in the Big Hall. He told us of the terrible dangers of the railway and how it was wrong to go across the lines on any account. And he told us how Albert had got run down by the Metal Train.

I never thought that Headmasters cried, but I could see the little stream of tears run from under his glasses.

Miss Webb was bad, too, and had to go out.

Playtime was very quiet that morning. Boxy Potter told

us all about it, because his brother was firing the engine.

They were just a mile below the school, on the 'down' line, and picking up speed for the gradient through the Cwm, when they saw the little figure running towards them up the track.

Billy Phipps, the Driver, pulled the brake hard.

'Sound the whistle!' he shouted to Boxy's brother.

When Boxy's brother pulled the cord, the steam blast echoed shrill down the track.

'Keep blowin', mun!' Billy Phipps was screaming as he dragged on the brake.

And Boxy's brother blew and blew.

He said Albert must have heard the whistle, because at the first blast he stopped, but he didn't leave the line. He just put his hands by his sides and stood perfectly still.

It took the Metal Train another quarter of a mile to halt.

Then they ran back up the line and found him.

We all missed Albert. School was never quite the same after that. There was no more War Effort Pile, and the Bowens gave up ink-drinking and got their pens back.

And Mr Pugh never blew a whistle at 'Lines' again. He just used to come and stand in the corner of the yard when it was time, and the boys would run quietly into order.

☆   ☆   ☆

Poor old Albert, if it hadn't been for those damned railway trucks, he might have been another Kenny Ball—Albert Portman and the Ink-Drinkers, a famous jazz band.

Well, if railway trucks had cut Albert's career short, I was damned sure they weren't going to ruin mine, even if they did look like *Bacillus anthracis*.

Vowing I would never make the same mistake again, I rolled over and went to sleep.

8

Win some—lose some. As the New Year progressed, my confidence returned. I was winning more than I was losing, my successes culminating in a prize that was, and has been ever since, the most priceless.

I married Diana in the spring.

During the months leading up to our wedding, several things happened that furthered my maturation from a 'green vet in Herefordshire pastures' to a 'Herefordshire vet in green pastures'. And there was no more formative a school for experience than the Granstone Estate, the home of Lord Pendleford and his sister, the Lady Octavia Grimes.

My first encounter with Her Ladyship had been the previous year, at Ledingford Show, which was held annually in the grounds of Granstone Castle, as were the Ledingford Hunt Point-to-Point, the Ledingford Carnival and several other county functions throughout the season.

While acting as Official Veterinary Surgeon at the Show, in the absence of Bob Hacker, I had had the somewhat delicate task of informing Lady Octavia that her goat, Bertie, entered in the Show, was an hermaphrodite, having both a 'willy' and a 'wonker' as Mr Bevan, Steward of the Goats, had put it.

Her Ladyship took the rejection of her favourite pet quite well. To everyone assembled, including myself, it was a profound relief when she declared the whole affair a 'hoot', and told me that the incident would brighten up the conversation at the After-Show dinner party, normally a stuffy affair, that her brother, Lord Pendleford, was giving that evening.

She had also invited me to call on her when I visited the Estate, as she bred Maltese and had over fifty of the perky little canines, and wished me to see her brood.

In fact, although I had since visited the Home Farm on several occasions, I had never gone along to the Castle's West Wing where she lived, and my first call was in the nature of a summons to attend Napoleon, her senior stud dog.

Granstone Castle stood in conspicuous grandeur, backed by a rise of woodland that sheltered its grey stone turrets from the north.

A high-walled battlement fronted the imposing edifice and, below, the terrain fell gently away to the river a mile or so beyond.

The oak-lined driveway to Granstone wound gently up the slope, in such a way that the incomer could not but fail to develop a certain degree of humility before passing through the lofty portals.

As I approached the entrance to the West Wing, I was reminded, oddly enough, of Park View at Abergranog, for although grander, the steps to the formidable oak door were equally steep. There was, of course, no faded sun curtain, but there was a letter box and I was sorely tempted to lift the flap and shout, 'Hugh with the meat!' When I rattled the great iron knocker, the echo from within also brought back memories of my Saturday errands and Aunty Dolly.

In fact, she possessed a vague similarity to Lady Octavia who, although taller and louder of voice, was adorned in an equal superfluity of powder, lipstick, bangles and beads.

When opened, however, the door did not reveal Her Ladyship. Instead, a sour-faced, grey-haired woman in a grubby jumper and skirt confronted me.

130

'Yes!' she said sharply.

'Hugh Lasgarn . . . the vet. I've come to see one of Lady Octavia's terriers.'

'Terriers!' she screeched, her eyes popping. 'Terriers!'

I have never, ever, since that day called Maltese anything other than Maltese. The look on that wretched woman's face and the sound of her voice were permanently imprinted upon my memory and, violent though my education was, it was most fortunate that I became cognisant of the correct terminology before meeting Her Ladyship. Her reaction to my ignorance was beyond contemplation.

Maltese are, of course, one of the oldest of the European Toy breeds, reference having been made to them, so Lady Octavia later informed me, by Aristotle, as coming from the island of Melita or Malta. In fact, as far back as 1763, when Sir Joshua Reynolds painted the then leading beauty, Nellie O'Brien, he showed her with a typical Maltese resting on her lap—and I'll wager that, even then, if he had called Nellie's pet a terrier he would never have finished the picture.

But my first sight of Maltese was frightening.

Mrs Gibbons, the housekeeper, led me along an austere passage, with doors at intervals on each side. On reaching the end, we passed into a large hallway, which in contrast was oak-panelled, with a large Jacobean 'When did you last see your father?' table in the centre.

Without any announcement, she turned the handles of the matching panelled doors and flung them open.

Beyond was a long, heavily furnished drawing-room, with rich tapestry armchairs, sofas and wall coverings. Vast gilt-framed oils hung on all sides and in the great open fireplace half a tree was burning—and everywhere were Maltese.

The chairs, the tables, window-sills, sofas, shelves and sideboards were covered with them, and when they saw

131

me, they advanced. I was set upon by a horde of white, fluffy, yapping dogs and a sea of canine commotion enveloped my feet.

They ragged my trousers and my socks, bit my shoes and undid my laces. They yelped and barked and jumped at my case, and even attempted to climb up my legs.

I stood rooted to the ground, my natural instincts for dealing with such a pack of jabbering fluffbags completely stifled, for beaming benevolently at her brood, as they endeavoured to devour my lower regions, was Lady Octavia, smoking a black cheroot and swinging what looked like a rosary in her other hand.

I forced a tolerant smile, wondering how long I was expected to stand there, for the noise was deafening and any comment a waste of time.

But Lady Octavia, in Boadicea fashion, quelled the riot with a voice that would have made the windows rattle in any less well constructed establishment.

'DESIST!' she cried.

As if by magic, the racket subsided and, like the biblical 'parting of the waves', the pack withdrew to either side, allowing me to enter.

'They've accepted you, Mr Lasgarn,' said Lady Octavia. 'I can tell.' She placed her cheroot in a large brass ashtray and, turning away, beckoned me to follow.

The pack moved as well, but with a command several decibels lower then the first, she steadied its progress.

Her Ladyship led me through a maze of passages and up several floors, eventually arriving at a narrow staircase, steep and rather dark.

Lady Octavia thumped up the thinly carpeted steps in her heavy brogues and, as I ascended behind, I noticed a series of framed etchings entitled 'The Harlot's Progress', running up the wall alongside. They were of a Rabelaisian character, each picture depicting a grotesque episode in the career of an adventurous and well-endowed lady. There

132

must have been about seven in all, and at each step the scenes became more interesting. Unfortunately, due to the lack of illumination, I could only make a guess at the last two, which momentarily took my mind away completely from the case in hand. On opening the door at the top, a shaft of light bore down upon us, but it came too late: I had arrived with Her Ladyship in what appeared to be an attic bedroom.

For a relatively small room, the furniture was large and ornate, in satin walnut, and in the centre stood a great square bed devoid of linen and pillows, but covered with a mountainous feather mattress.

In the central depression lay the Little Emperor himself: Napoleon of Granstone—the Senior Stud.

For one carrying such a title, Napoleon was a disappointment, for he was limp and lifeless, his eyes tired, and occasionally he shivered, even though he was wearing a grey woollen jersey, the same colour as Mrs Gibbons' but considerably less grubby.

'Mr Lasgarn's come to see you, Nappy,' shouted Lady Octavia, as if addressing an aged and deaf relative. 'He's going to see if he can pep you up, eh!' She sat down, side-saddle, on the feather mattress and stroked his fluffy top-knot, which was tied with a red ribbon.

'Rarely have you folks to my lot,' she said. 'Odd whelping and a couple of broken legs, about all I've needed any help with for years.'

'Vaccinations against Distemper?' I queried.

'Good God, no. Don't believe in all that rubbish. Regular fasting one day a week and garlic and fenugreek every day. Nothing like it. Take 'em meself, don't you know!'

I didn't know but I could well imagine, and wondered why I had, indeed, been summoned.

Lady Octavia explained.

'Nappy here is eight years old and normally is like a little lion. Right on top of his job, produces some fine litters and has never for a day been sick or sorry. That is, until a few months ago.' The little dog rested his head upon his paws, as if he had heard it all before. 'Well,' she continued, 'the old chap had had rather a busy session; he was on Kola pills to give him the old spark and, when he finished, I put him on a course of Highland Fling.' She went to a drawer in a dressing table, took out a large bottle and, unscrewing the cap, poured a clutch of small green tablets into her palm.

'Try one!' she ordered.

'What are they?' I asked, taken aback at being medicated myself before I had even examined my patient.

'A compound of vegetables, secret formula. Have them sent down from the north of Scotland. Go on, man. They won't kill you!'

I only had her word for it, but Lady Octavia was a very persuasive person and, as it was my first visit, I didn't want to arouse any dissent. I took one.

It was dry and crumbly and tasted of concentrated cabbage. Lady Octavia gave one to Napoleon, which he appeared to consume with relish, and popped the rest in her own mouth; then she replaced the lid and put the bottle back on the dressing table.

'I've used them for years,' she continued. 'Normally they get him back to his old form in a few weeks—but not this time. So I doubled his dose, but still he was listless and didn't seem to have any energy at all. He ate, but not with his usual gusto. Then, about a month ago, it started . . .'

Her Ladyship leaned forward and undid the buttons on Napoleon's woollen jersey and, when she rolled it back, I could understand her concern, for Napoleon of Granstone, the Senior Stud, was as naked as a skinned rabbit.

Poor little devil, I thought, no wonder he was shivering. He looked up at me sadly, as if acutely embarrassed by his affliction, and, indeed, I felt sorry for him, for he did look a pathetic sight.

'Just started to come out like a normal moult,' said Lady Octavia. 'Groomed him and groomed him, but the more I did, the more it came out. And now look at him!'

A close examination of Nappy's skin revealed no obvious abnormality; in fact, apart from being bald, I could find nothing wrong at all. There was no sign of infection, mange, fleas or lice. I was tempted to suggest that, with close on fifty wives, his hair might have fallen out with worry, but it was obviously no occasion for humour.

'Now, what do you think, Mr Lasgarn?' asked Lady Octavia.

I countered by questioning her on the details of the feeding regime, exercise, hygiene and general habits, and could fault nothing. It was no good suggesting vitamins, for Lady Octavia had included them from A to Z—if there was a 'Z'.

It was the revolting taste of the cabbage tablet that triggered off the clue. The Brassica group of plants, including kale and cabbage, has been known to contain a goitrogenic factor that, in some cases, can affect the thyroid gland.

'Has he been losing weight?' I asked.

'Surprisingly enough, no,' she replied. 'That's why I wasn't too concerned.'

I took a second and more intense look at Napoleon's skin and discovered at the base of his neck and on his hind-quarters a very slight scaliness that I had missed before. The only other differential diagnosis would have been a testicular abnormality, but I had checked that at my first examination, and although Napoleon was bald, his masculinity was in no doubt.

It was a long shot, but I could think of no other condition that fitted the symptoms. 'Be not afraid,' Professor Jennings had said, although he had never met Lady Octavia; I took his advice and explained my conclusion.

'I think Napoleon has developed hypothyroidism,' I announced.

135

Her Ladyship sat quite still, then raised her eyebrows and said: 'Tell me more, Mr Lasgarn. Tell me more.'

I expected an interrogative and argumentative session to follow, but instead she listened intently, without comment, until I had finished, stroking Nappy's top-knot all the while. Then she nodded her head several times and, to my relief and no little surprise, said, 'You're probably right, Mr Lasgarn. You're probably right.'

I explained that the hair loss and weight gain might be counteracted by the use of a thyroid extract—although the dosage was variable and results would have to be carefully observed.

I told her that I would never have countenanced such a treatment, but for the fact that I knew she was highly experienced in the use of natural medicaments; and that thyroxin, although being of animal origin, was still a natural product and, in my opinion, as acceptable, in principle, as any herbal remedy.

I cast no aspersions upon the Highland Fling, but told her that the tablets should be discontinued.

From her facial expression, I sensed she concurred with my every statement.

Throughout the whole dissertation, I did not delude myself as to my tactics and was well aware of my emphasis upon Her Ladyship's homoeopathic capabilities—and I could see that the flattery was very effective.

The art of veterinary medicine is not dead! I told myself, and promised to post the tablets that very day.

At that moment, there came a clattering on the stairs and the door was flung open—it was Mrs Gibbons.

'Peel's at the door, ma'am. Wants to see Mr Lasgarn. Urgent!'

'See Mr Lasgarn!' countered Her Ladyship. 'He's attending to Napoleon. How dare he!'

'It's Kismet, ma'am. There's something wrong with him.'

'Oh!' Lady Octavia rose from her seat on the feather

mattress. 'Oh. That's different.'

She could see I was puzzled, so she explained:

'Kismet is my brother, Lord Pendleford's hunter—well, one of them, but his favourite. He's away shooting in Gloucestershire, and Crabb, the Head Groom, is in hospital having his veins done—and a damned inconvenient time, too. You'd better go, Mr Lasgarn. Peel's a good boy, but young, and that horse is everything to Lord Pendleford.'

Peel was standing at the door, cap in hand; he was about seventeen, fresh-faced and rather scrawny.

'He's up on Larch Track,' he blurted out anxiously when he saw me. 'Won't move. Don' think he's lame, but he's sweating like a pig. But I never pushed him, just hacked him, gentle, from Home Farm, then up the ride, when all of a sudden he pulled up short. I seen your car 'ere, when I went by, so I've left him with the woodman and come on down.'

From the tarmacadam road that ran behind the Big House and across the length of the estate, were several tracks leading up into the woods.

Larch Track was only a few minutes' walk away, but Peel walked quickly and, with case in hand, I found the going a bit rough.

Eventually, we came to a clearing and, standing there, with the woodman loosely holding his reins, was Kismet, a dark mahogany bay, seventeen hands if he was an inch. He certainly was a fine looking animal, quality horseflesh through and through.

'Ain't shifted since you left,' said the woodman to Peel. 'But sweat—comin' out of 'im by the bucket—an' 'e's bin passin' blood in 'is water!'

'Christ!' exclaimed Peel. ' 'E isn't going to die, is 'e?'

I didn't answer, for at that point I didn't know.

'Gelding?' I asked.

Peel nodded.

'How old?'

137

'Rising nine,'

'Any trouble before?'

'Naw. Tough as old boots, an' go all day, normally. Odd cuts and bruises, but that's all.'

'Feeding?'

'Corning him well—it's the season,' the boy replied.

'And how about exercise?' I asked.

'As well as hunting they all get about five miles a day, regular. Well . . .' he hesitated. 'I've had to cut down a bit with Mr Crabb away, I can't get round it all.'

'Cut down—how much?'

'Well, there's four altogether. I can take two at a time with the others. But old Kizzy 'ere is an independent old devil, so I've got to take 'im by 'imself and 'e missed a couple of days over the weekend.'

'And you still corned him?'

The boy nodded. 'He'll eat his grub any time.'

I took my stethoscope and listened to Kismet's heart. It was racing, even though he was at rest, and his pulse, which I took on the brachial artery, just inside his foreleg, was rapid and soft. His whole body was tense and his eyes reflected a nervous apprehension, while occasionally he looked back at his flanks, as if confused by his immobility.

'Is it a stroke?' asked Peel.

I ran my hand over Kismet's sweating hindquarters; they were 'board-hard' and in spasm.

It was a classic case of 'azoturia'.

Monday Morning Disease, Set-fast or Tying-up, were all names for the same syndrome, although azoturia was the more severe form of Monday Morning Disease, so called because in the days when there were far more work-horses about, it was often seen after a weekend's rest.

The condition resulted from the high carbohydrate diet that Kismet had been having in the form of a large corn ration. This diet produced a significant storage of 'animal starch' or glycogen in the muscles, which, under normal conditions, was worked off with exercise. But being stabled, the 'animal starch' had increased excessively and the sudden resumption of training, instead of breaking it down into glucose or 'blood sugar', a readily available form of energy, produced lactic acid instead. This unfortunate by-product, being very irritant, had caused muscle damage, especially over the large muscle groups of the hindquarters.

Hence the reason why Kismet was sweating over the rump and in obvious pain.

The rupture of the muscle cells releases a red substance called myoglobin which passes around the body in the blood stream. Eventually it is filtered through the kidneys, producing the reddened urine that the woodman had seen.

In severe cases, the deposits of this muscle substance could cause kidney damage that might permanently impair the health and performance of the unfortunate victim.

I explained my diagnosis and the suspected cause to Peel.

'The cold weather could have made things worse,' I commented. 'He wants rugging up as soon as possible.'

'How'll we get him home?' asked Peel.

'You can't,' I said. 'Not until the acid has cleared his system; until then, any excess movement will increase the muscle damage. What's in there?' I motioned to a small cabin about fifty yards up the track.

'The old charcoal hut,' said the woodman. 'Ain't bin used for years—but it's sound enough an' the roof's good.'

'My advice is to put him in there,' I said. 'Rest him for twenty-four hours, then box him back to Home Farm. He'll need four or five days' rest, even after that.'

'Goin' to bleed 'im?' asked the woodman. 'Purge 'em, bleed 'em and sling 'em—that's what they used to do.'

'You've seen it before, then,' I said, surprised at his remarks.

'Lord! When my Father was ostler 'ere, when they 'ad thirty an' more workin' 'orses, you could guarantee one or two at the beginning of every week. Old Mr Blandson was the vet then, real toff. "Bold dose of aloes, a basin of blood an' the weight off their legs!" he'd say. Always worked.'

'Well, there'll be no blood-letting today,' I said, opening my case. 'I'll give Kismet something to ease the pain, then he wants warming up and a good bran mash.'

'I'll chuck my jacket over him for now,' said Peel, undoing the girth and slipping off the tack. 'Then I'll go back down and get the rest.' He slapped the great bay affectionately under the neck. 'He will get better, Mr Lasgarn, won't he? If anything happens to 'm, His Lordship will hang me, but apart from that, it is my fault an it would break my heart, too. He's such a grand old fella.'

'I think your neck is safe,' I told him. 'You were right not to move him, and that has more than likely saved a disaster. He should be a lot better by tomorrow, but you'll have to watch him from now on; once they've had it, it can recur.'

We walked Kismet to the charcoal hut, which made a reasonable stable, and I checked over again that Peel knew exactly what to do.

'Bed him down, rug him and massage his hindquarters. A bran mash only and make sure he's got water. I'll call first thing tomorrow, but don't move him until I've been.'

I felt quite elated as I drove away from Granstone and was secretly pleased with my diagnostic prowess—two unusual cases within the hour—and gratified to think that practice was not just lame cows and calvings; there was a lot more to test one's capabilities, even in rural Herefordshire.

That evening, McBean and I went for a drink at the Hopman Arms, which we often did when the work of the day was concluded.

The pub was crowded and our usual corner taken. As we stood waiting to be served, McBean asked what I had been up to.

'Went to Granstone today,' I replied.

'Aha! An' how did ye get on?' he asked, one eye on the

barmaid.

'Diagnosed hypothyroidism in Her Ladyship's stud dog and azoturia in His Lordship's hunter,' I announced proudly.

'An' my arse is a violet!' said McBean, catching the barmaid's eye at last. 'Two pints, me darlin!' he shouted. 'One for me, an' one for Professor Hugh Lasgarn, here. If you please!'

9

The floral qualities of McBean's *derrière*, were of little consequence, for what really mattered was that Napoleon responded, albeit slowly, to my recommended treatment and Kismet appeared to have made a complete recovery.

Lord Pendleford was particularly impressed by my handling of his horse, for being a hunting man and knowledgeable about equine matters, he appreciated the significance of the action I had taken, which, although relatively simple, was vital to Kismet's recovery.

So impressed was His Lordship that he invited me to the Tenants' Shoot, to be held at Granstone on the last Saturday of the season.

I had done a bit of rough shooting at John Carpenter's, a pal of mine who ran a small dairy farm.

My first visit to his place caught him unprepared and in the middle of milking, so he lent me his gun and said:

'Go and take a walk around for an hour—I'll be ready when you get back.'

Since then, I had spent several Saturday afternoons at his place, rough shooting, and although the bag was never very large, I found the necessary concentration and subsequent stimulation such a contrast to my daily routine that it was a welcome break.

'Granstone, eh!' commented Bob Hacker, obviously impressed at my entry into 'High Society'.

'It's only the Tenants' Shoot,' I replied.

'They have Royalty there in the season,' said Bob. 'One of the finest shoots in the West of England, is Granstone.'

'Any tips?' I asked, for I knew Bob to be a good marksman who had been game shooting for years.

'What are you doing for a gun?'

'I thought I'd ask John Carpenter.'

'You can borrow one of mine,' he offered generously. 'Now, tips. Let's see.' He scratched the back of his neck with his index finger.

'Remember to swing through; too many birds are lost behind. And if you have to think whether it's in range— don't shoot; because unless you're top class, by the time you've made up your mind, the bird's too far away for a clean kill. Stick to your peg and remember the rules of the line. Oh, and don't drink too much port at lunch!'

It was sound advice and, in due course, with Bob's twelve-bore Baxter, a belt full of Number Fives and, optimistically, a game bag, I arrived at Granstone at ten o'clock on a drizzly Saturday morning.

We assembled on the battlements, where Lord Pendleford himself passed round a tray of 'starters'—sloe gin, that ran like a red hot poker, straight to my stomach.

There were fifteen guns in all, each well equipped and very cheery. I knew several who were clients of ours; there was Clampton of The Dyke, the Powell brothers, Dick Wilsden and Bill Small, the Landlord of the 'Shoes and a local corn merchant. The others had familiar faces, but I didn't know their names.

All seemed to own dogs, which made me feel a trifle inadequate; for if anybody should have a dog, it ought to be the vet, I thought.

The dogs knew what it was all about and treated the occasion as a social gathering, very much like their owners. Some, mostly the Springers, were extrovert and eager to make friends, whilst others remained more aloof. Of the latter, the Yellow Labradors seemed to be the biggest snobs.

Lord Pendleford's Head Keeper, Ben Watson, was

standing thoughtfully by, weighing up the talent. Not that a Tenants' Shoot was any less 'quality' than a Gentlemen's Shoot when it came to expertise—and, in many cases, the bag could be considerably more.

To me, a keeper's life appeared a constant enigma.

Rearing and caring for the birds, vigorously guarding them against predators, nurturing them through the vagaries of the weather, jealously protecting their haunts and feeding places . . . then, come the season, after encouraging their feathery trust and confidence, driving them to their slaughter.

What hypocrisy!

But in fact gamekeepers, I later came to realise, were somewhat maligned and much-suffering people, for their job was about as difficult as any in a country parish. The village policeman's task was simple by comparison, for at least he had right on his side, and even the most rebellious villagers would not dare deny his usefulness as a keeper of the peace.

The keeper of the Squire's pheasant and partridge, however, in many eyes served no useful purpose.

Amongst the older generation who, in some cases, still retained memories of an empty belly and a meagre grate, the injustice of having to allow game to strut about their gardens when the pot was empty, preserved old enmities. Any attempt to take a bird could well result in an appearance before the Bench, where the Squire himself would exact full and sometimes harsh retribution.

But somewhere in the back of my mind there was, too, the grim memory of a scene I had chanced upon when I was a boy.

We had gone for a car ride to the country in Jack Knight's new Austin Seven. We stopped near Monmouth and, while Jack and my father stood admiring the car and Mother and Mrs Knight gossiped away, I wandered into a nearby wood.

It was so peaceful as I meandered up the sunny green ride, with the haunting scent of the damp woodland filling the air; pure bliss—until I turned the corner.

There, hanging head downwards on a horizontal ash-pole, were stoats and weasels, along with magpies and jays, their gay wings wet and broken, infested with insects that had seized upon their sad decay.

The sight printed itself indelibly upon my youthful mind; to me it was not only shocking, but senseless.

I ran back in stumbling fashion to tell the grown-ups, but they just said it was a 'Keeper's Gibbet', and went on talking.

Yet, here I was at Granstone . . . Who was the hypocrite now?

Everyone in the shooting party seemed relaxed and confident, and I hoped that I would be put somewhere completely inconspicuous.

When we drew for stands, I turned up 'Fifteen'; that was bound to be miles away, and I breathed a sigh of relief.

Lord Pendleford announced that he would not be accompanying us due to 'the old leg', but said he would join up at lunch and wished us all 'good sport'.

Two Land Rovers were standing by for the guns, the beaters having already gone ahead.

'Victoria Wood first, gentlemen!' shouted Watson. 'One to six in the front. Seven to twelve behind.'

The party divided, and guns and dogs piled into their alloted vehicles, amid much commotion and excited barking.

Three of us, Bill Small, another youngish chap and myself were left, standing together.

'Mr Small and Mr Smithson, you're down on the Park,' said Watson, coming over and pointing to below the battlements. 'And, Mr Lasgarn, it's your lucky day.' He looked at me and smiled. 'You won't have to walk far, you're over

145

there.' And he pointed to a hazel stick with a white card pinned to it—smack in the middle of the great lawn, right in front of the house.

My heart sank to my boots and I was about to protest, when he continued:

'They come high from the back and make for the Crib.' He pointed to a small coppice, below in the distance. 'Wait for the whistle, if you please, gentlemen. Good luck.'

Then, he jumped into the passenger seat of the rear vehicle and away they went. Bill Small and Smithson disappeared down the steps to the Park and I was left on the vast green apron—all alone.

I felt sick and wished I had never come.

The drizzle had eased, leaving a grey, still day, transforming the woodland I was facing into a dense concourse of trunks and branches. A dull, deep, secretive repository for my unsuspecting prey. It was depressing, so I turned away and looked down over the sloping acres to the river.

From Abergranog Council School to Granstone Castle was a big jump—no matter how one did it.

'If they could see me, now,' I hummed, thinking of Wendel, Boxy Potter and the rest. Not that they hadn't moved on, for Wendel had got to Cambridge on a scholarship and taken a First in Zoology, and Boxy was a mining engineer. Education alone was not the passport to transcending the class barriers, and yet a vet had a unique opportunity to achieve just that. The basic human concern for animals, and the need for them, not only for food, lowered everyone's guard, prince and pauper alike—and the country vet was there to see it.

Suddenly, I heard the whistle, shrill and clear, and my heart leaped.

Within the misty depths of the woodland bank erupted the sound of the beaters as they called and thrashed

146

through the undergrowth.

I 'broke' the gun and slid two cartridges into place; then, fingering the safety catch, I took a deep breath.

Like baying hounds, the beaters approached. It was unnerving, yet my whole body tingled with a sense of sharp anticipation—ears straining to pick up the first frantic flutter, eyes fixed for any movement.

Abruptly, a shot rang out, but before its rolling echo had died away there was another, and another, then a regular cannonade.

The birds were leaving the wood, but despite the obviously considerable flush, none came my way—and I was glad.

Then all went quiet and, in spite of my previous sentiments, I regretted not having had the opportunity for a shot. The beaters were quite close, although I could not see them, and I glanced to my left to pick up the positions of Bill Small and Smithson.

As I turned back I saw him—a great, dark-feathered cock pheasant—flailing the air with his powerful wings, neck stretched and tail feathers curved upwards to give him height.

He was rising fast and overhead, aiming to reach a point where he could glide swiftly and safely down to the Crib.

He was past me quickly and over my left shoulder, still rising. It was lucky that my balance was good, my feet spread so that I could pivot smoothly, the gun coming up as I did.

Perfect action is not rapid and jerky, but flowing and gentle, like an artist brushing a backward stroke, an exercise with feeling, even empathy.

I took him at his highest point, as he momentarily hung in the misty air before tightening his tail to float away.

One second he was poised to escape, a beautiful, flying bird, the next, neck bent and over on his back, he fell in a vertical line, like a weighted feather duster.

I didn't see him land, for he disappeared out of sight,

below the battlements.

But I heard the chill thump as his body hit the turf.

I shall always remember the thrill of my first pheasant. Perhaps it satisfied the basic primaeval urge of man, the hunter. No, satisfying is not the word, for the true sensation was indescribable.

And although, years later, I was to change my attitude towards the sport, I never regretted that day. For one can only hold realistic and worthwhile opinions if one knows both sides—as I was to learn in the coming weeks.

☆　　☆　　☆

The Ledingford Hunt held its annual Point-to-Point meeting on the last day of February on the Park at Granstone. It was extremely well supported and, as the Hunt had most of its country in our practice, many of the members were also clients.

As as result, the Hacker Practice acted as Honorary Veterinary Surgeons at the meeting, and it was usual for Bob Hacker to attend. However, on the Thursday of that week Bob, who was a member of the British Veterinary Association Council, discovered he was expected to attend an important session that weekend.

Saturday afternoon should have been my free time, but due to the unexpected arrangement, he asked me if I would go to Granstone.

'You'll find it interesting, Hugh,' he remarked encouragingly. 'You'll know quite a lot of folk there, anyway. The going could be a bit heavy, though,' he added, looking through the window at the overcast sky. 'Granstone is an uphill course and a good test, even on a dry day. Usually there's a fair field, a lot just having a run, and not really racing fit; but then, I suppose it is the first meeting around these parts and they're all eager to get at it.'

'What sort of problems am I likely to come up against?' I

asked, a trifle apprehensively.

'At point-to-points it's often from one extreme to the other,' Bob replied. 'Minor cuts and sprains to broken bones; but, as Hon Vet, you're there just to give first aid— patch 'em up and send them home.'

'What kit should I need?' I asked.

'Oh, usual stuff. I don't normally reckon to stitch cuts if I can help it—unless they are really gaping, that is. Horses are very prone to 'proud flesh', and what may look like a neat piece of embroidery at the time can turn out a real cobbled job when it heals. Pack the wounds with sulphona-mide and bandage if you can. You may get a few bleeders,' he continued, scratching his chin, thoughtfully, 'though mostly they've stopped by the time you've found them. Then, of course, there's the broken legs and backs. Haven't had any trouble that way for the last two seasons, but a few years ago, I had to shoot three—all in one afternoon. Have you used the Greener?'

I shook my head.

Bob bent down, unlocked a drawer in his desk and brought out the humane killer—a Greener 310 and a box of cartridges.

It was an odd-looking instrument, nothing like a gun. In fact, it appeared just an innocuous piece of pipe, with a sloping disc at one end and a plunger at the other.

Bob unscrewed the plunger.

'Bullet in here,' he pointed to the inlet. 'Screw the cap back on. So!' He twisted the plunger back into position. 'Hold it in the palm. So!' He clasped it in his left hand like a dumb-bell. Then he took a small metal weight. 'And when in position on the head, hit it. So!'

He hit the plunger sharply with the weight and although it was not loaded, the gun gave an ominous click.

'Shoot 'em high,' he continued, in a matter-of-fact way. 'This'll drop 'em okay. But remember that a horse's brain presents a relatively small area to the front and, due to the shape of the skull, the approach is limited, so you must be accurate. Top centre at a line with the poll strap—and, for God's sake, clear all bystanders out of the way. A ricochet from this little demon is lethal at fifty yards.'

He chatted on about some of the likely runners and who owned them—but I was standing cold and unnerved. It was the first time I had seen a Greener and the prospect of shooting a horse in public sickened me.

How odd that, just a few weeks previously, I had been standing surveying the Park at Granstone and shooting for pleasure—and now, when it was part of my job, I felt shocked. I just didn't want to be involved.

'Old Brettner will be there,' Bob was saying. 'They invite both practices. You've met him, haven't you?'

I shook my head again.

'It'll either be him or his assistant. Don't know his assistant or what he's like, but the old man himself won't be a lot of help. Enjoys the hospitality too much.' Bob mimed raising a glass to his lips. 'But at least you know where to find him!'

He gave me a badge, a race card and a car pass.

'First race, one-thirty,' he said. 'Best get there about one. See Jerry Carling—he's Clerk of the Course—an' he'll put you right. Okay?' he looked up questioningly.

I nodded.

'You'll enjoy it, Hugh,' he concluded, getting up from his desk. 'Great fun!'

'Thanks,' I said, but inwardly, I had my doubts.

The entrance to the Point-to-Point was near the river, on the side opposite to Granstone Castle, which looked down upon the course from the top of the ridge about three-quarters of a mile away.

There were nine fences in all: some natural, over reinforced parts of growing hedge, whilst others were prefabricated, consisting of tight brushwood and standing independently, on open ground.

It struck me, when I drove in, as being a very cosmopolitan affair, with country, county and town all mingling together in a gaggle of colour, movement and noise. The predominantly brown and green tweedy dress-wear blended with the late winter shades of the natural countryside, broken only, but in sharp relief, by the brightly coloured silks and jerseys of the riders.

Sheepskin-coated, head-scarved, shrieking women stalked about, accompanied by trilbied, narrow-faced, hacking-jacketed men with oversize binocular cases strapped to their bodies. In the beer tent, the townies, amid peels of raucous laughter, pushed and shoved towards the bar.

The air was full of the intense chatter and banter of the bookies on their stands, their voices competing with the tannoy as it crackled out an interminable flurry of unintelligible information.

Yet, amid all the babble and frantic action, stood the horses, heads held high and looking about, as if they knew full well that they were the true VIPs; that superiority was a matter of deciding who, amongst themselves, was the strongest and fastest; humans, although present, were superfluous when it really came down to it.

'Great fun!' Bob Hacker had said, and it certainly looked it—although for my part, I felt tense.

I found the Secretary's tent and the Clerk of the Course, Jerry Carling.

'Jolly good!' he exclaimed, shaking my hand vigorously. 'See you've got your badge. There's a Land Rover somewhere, if you need to go out into the country. Hope you don't have too many disasters to deal with. Any problems, see me!' Then he turned away to deal with someone else. I was just about to leave, when he added: 'Mr Brettner's here. Saw him a minute ago!'

As I stood outside the tent, deciding which direction I

should take, my eye fell on a stocky figure with a loud check cap, military-style overcoat, narrow trousers, shiny red boots and a face to match—and on his lapel was pinned a blue badge, similar to mine.

I walked across.

'Mr Brettner?'

He looked up from the race card he had been studying.

'Hugh Lasgarn—with Hacker's.'

When he raised his head, I could see he was wearing gold-rimmed half-spectacles, over the top of which he peered at me in a rather studious fashion.

Without a word, he studied may face intently for several seconds, then he ran his eye down the right arm of my duffle, to the case I was holding. From there, along to my left pocket, from which protruded my stethoscope—then back to my face.

'Mm. Ready for action, eh? Good for you!' Then he held out his hand in greeting. 'Fancy a "warmer"?'

It was a bit early in the meeting to start drinking, but I didn't want to appear unsociable.

'I'd like to get my bearings first,' I said. 'Have a look round.'

'I've been here enough times to know my bearings,' he replied. 'We'll probably meet up later. I'll be over there if you want me—'he nodded across to the Members' Tent. Then, slapping his palm with the race card, he took a step closer and we stood practically face to face. 'First time, is it?' He dropped his voice to a confidential whisper. I nodded. 'Just a tip, then. If they call for the vet, don't go off at a bloody gallop; a slow trot is as much as you'll need.' He winked over the top of his gold-rimmed specs, flicked my shoulder with the card and set off for his 'warmer'.

There were no incidents on the course during the first three races, although the fields were strong and the pace fast for the conditions. Quite a few riders were unseated and several pulled up—but no 'disasters', and I began to relax a little and even enjoy the atmosphere.

I was called to the unsaddling enclosure to a bay mare with a nose-bleed that obligingly stopped before I got there; at another incident, the horse in question, with a reported sprained tendon, was being busily treated by a young woman in skin-tight jods, who seemed to resent that I had been called at all.

It was in the fifth race—the Open—that the 'disaster' occurred.

The distance was three-and-a-half miles, just over two circuits of the course: the big race of the afternoon.

Lord Pendleford's Kismet was among the twelve entries and, with young Peel in the saddle, they looked a grand turn-out. As they walked down to the start, I felt a thrill of pride and pleasure run through my bones, that the magnificent animal had responded to my veterinary care.

The start was orderly and, in view of the distance, nobody keen to make the running. When they came round for the first time, they had kept just about the same order, with Kismet lying ninth, but going easily.

When it happened, I didn't actually see the whole incident. Three fences from home on the second circuit, a tight group of horses, about five, seemed to take the fence together in a bunch, the leader pecking as he landed.

It was a just a second or so, then he recovered. But it was time enough momentarily to upset the followers, who were all in mid-air.

They all landed short, and a single horse, coming fast behind, piled into the back of them.

All except the last one miraculously kept their feet and scrambled away. Then someone moved in front of me and, when I looked again, I could see a horse lying on the ground.

'There's a faller!' A man shouted behind me. 'Real cropper.'

'Ain't movin',' said another. 'Jockey's up, though!'

It was too far to pick out even the colour of the horse clearly, and the crowd's attention was taken again by the oncoming racers. But one man still had his binoculars trained on the accident. I was standing right behind him. For a few seconds he followed the approaching bunch, then he dropped his hands.

'It's the favourite, all right, that's gone!'

'The favourite, which one is that?'

His reply knocked me cold.

'Kismet, of course. His Lordship's horse . . . an' he looks bad, too!'

I doubled back to the tent where I had left my case and, grabbing it, looked anxiously about for the Land Rover. I couldn't spot one handy. The crowd were now frantically cheering home the winner, but over their heads in the distance, I could see others running out to the fallen horse, so I set off towards them, quickly.

The going was quite hard and, with my duffle coat on, I soon became hot and breathless. In the back of my mind I remembered old Brettner's advice—but heeded it not.

It was truly amazing where all the folks had come from, for although I was fast to the scene, already there were thirty or more gathered round.

I should have been able to shout authoritatively, 'Stand back! I'm the vet!' But I was too puffed and just barged my way to the front.

At the sight of my bag and stethoscope the crowd eased, and I came upon a white-faced Peel, kneeling at Kismet's head, with tears in his eyes.

'Broke 'is back,' said a burly individual. 'Wants putting out of 'is misery.'

I glared at the outspoken know-all, but made no comment as I attempted to assess poor Kismet's condition.

The bay was lying on his right side, all four legs stretched

154

out stiffly, his sleek coat lathered in sweat. The breathing was shallow, with nostrils flaring as occasional shivers ran the length of his prostrate body. But the most distressing symptom was the low groan that he gave periodically—a deep, agonising, throaty groan, as if he was on the point of expiring.

'Don' let 'm suffer!' shouted a voice from the back, together with one or two other emotive comments which I tried to ignore.

Peel looked up, his face drawn with anguish.

'Is 'e a gonner, Mr Lasgarn?'

'I don't know,' I said, stalling. 'I haven't had a chance to examine him yet.'

But in my heart I suspected the worst.

The accurate diagnosis of racecourse injuries is never easy. Apart from the obvious lack of X-ray facilities, the pressure of being in the public eye under such emotive conditions, with excitable onlookers and distressed owners, can challenge even the coolest professional.

And to someone like me, at that moment, it was devastating.

My mind went completely blank—I didn't know where to begin.

I knelt down beside Peel, and he started to describe what had happened. So I concentrated on listening to him, in an attempt to detach myself from the surrounding panic and the thirty pairs of eyes on my back.

'His Lordship said: "Keep out of trouble and come from behind on the run in," 'he began, falteringly. 'He was goin' like a dream, an' I knew he had it all in 'im for the last few furlongs. But it was my fault.' He stroked Kismet's sweating forehead gently. 'My fault. He'd been clearin' them so well that I missed to look for trouble ahead, an' we come over right on top of the bunch. His back legs caught the fence 'ard, and he splayed and crashed down, smack on 'is belly.'

I felt a cold sweat coming over me, despite my warmth,

for Peel's description was the classic fall for a thoraco-lumbar fracture—a break in the middle of the back.

Kismet was still groaning and I took my stethoscope to listen to his heart. It was banging away furiously, although his pulse, when I felt it, was rapid and weak.

With a hypodermic needle, I pricked the lower limbs to test his reflexes. They were poor, although, with the shivering fits, it was difficult to decide how poor.

As I stood up, a Land Rover Estate arrived and out got Lord Pendleford and his secretary, a weasely individual called Withers.

'Lasgarn!' His Lordship acknowledged me, then looked down at his horse. 'How is he?' he asked, without raising his head.

'Very shocked,' I said.

'Broken back?' he asked, sharply.

'I don't know, M'Lord,' I replied. 'It's difficult to tell.'

'Don't want him to suffer, Lasgarn. Do what you think fit.'

'He's well insured, Your Lordship,' whined Withers at his side.

Lord Pendleford spun round on his secretary. 'Damn your eyes, man!' he exploded in a fury. 'That horse, to me, is priceless! Irreplaceable! To hell with the money!' He rounded upon me. 'I'll not have him in pain, d'ye hear?'

At that point, Kismet gave another low moan and the eyes of the crowd, once again, burned into me.

I crossed over to my case and, kneeling down, unlatched the lid.

'Clear the crowd and shoot them high', was Bob Hacker's advice.

How different from my last sporting occasion at Granstone. All alone then, just myself and a cock pheasant. That was pleasure—so-called—and this was work. Yet both were killing. It just didn't make sense.

My hand shook as I pulled open the large bottom drawer,

156

in which lay the Greener.

As I put my fingers around its cold steel barrel and was about to lift it out, there came a shuffling sound from behind. Then a grunt, a snort, a high-pitched whinny and, as I half turned from my crouched position, I saw Kismet raise his head.

Then, to my amazement and absolute relief, he shook himself and rolled onto his brisket. Throwing his head back and nearly bowling Peel over, the bay gelding pushed his forelegs out ahead of him and rose onto his hindquarters. He sat there for a few seconds, then stood on all fours and shook himself vigorously.

'Winded!' roared Lord Pendleford, raising two clenched fists in the air. 'Thank God for that!'

'Thank God, indeed!' I murmured to myself and, closing the drawer, rose to my feet, more shakily than Kismet.

The crowd started to disperse, some relieved at the recovery, a few disappointed that there was to be no more dramatic a spectacle.

'He'll be all right, now, Lasgarn,' said His Lordship confidently.

'You'll have to walk him back home very slowly,' I advised.

'Peel shall wait here with him,' he said. 'I'll go off and get a box arranged.' Then, after giving his horse a comforting pat on the neck, he got into the Land Rover, Withers scuttling in beside him, and they drove away.

'Just come at the right time. Everything okay?'

I turned to find Mr Brettner, hands deep in the pockets of his military overcoat, standing behind.

'Winded, thank God!' I exclaimed. 'Had me rattled for a bit.'

'Always take your time, lad,' he said, wagging his finger at me. 'Gentle trot—remember. Me . . . at my age, it's just a walk.'

I was forced to smile at last. 'You're right.' I agreed. 'And

I certainly wouldn't have enjoyed shooting that horse.'

'Enjoyed shooting!' retorted Brettner, gruffly. 'Lasgarn! Any vet who shoots for enjoyment is like an upholsterer who slashes furniture for fun!'

He looked at me severely over his half-specs. And as I picked up my case I thought to myself that although Josiah Brettner might have had a reputation for being a bit of a soak, the old vet spoke a lot of truth.

'Come on,' he wheezed. 'Let's go and have a "warmer".'

And with that experience under my belt, I decided that a 'warmer' was a very good idea.

☆   ☆   ☆

It was McBean who maintained that vets drove cars as others rode horses, and that if you ever saw vet's car in a hedge, it was probably because he had forgotten he was on the Queen's Highway and thought he was at a Point-to-Point.

LCJ 186, my little sit-up-and-beg Ford, had been a faithful mount for me for two years, but, like an old horse, sadly it had to come to the end of its days. During its long, adventurous career, having been in McBean's hands before mine, practically all its moving parts had been renewed several times. But now the bodywork was failing and the little Ford and I had to part company.

I owed it a lot for transporting me safely all those miles, and perhaps it seemed odd that, as a vet, I should become attached to an inanimate piece of metallic junk—for that was all it was at the end. But there was one particular debt of gratitude that I quite openly admitted to owing it, and that was for starting on a damp night, when a very much posher and up-market MG coupé failed to fire, and I gave a lift to a young lady whom, in one week's time, I was going to marry.

In its place I was given a new car, a dove-grey Ford Anglia of modern design, with red upholstery and registered OVJ

276.

I was, of course, thrilled with it. It seemed so low and sleek after my other car that my ego clicked up several notches as I drove it from the garage.

I decided to collect it on an afternoon when I had but one call—a small tuberculin test, about seven animals at Mr Jones, The Derry.

I purred through the countryside feeling like Lord Pendleford himself, but when I started up the narrow winding road to The Derry, I became rather nervous lest some mad farmer on a brakeless tractor should come rattling around the bend.

There was a gravelled clearing halfway up the hill by the wood, where the foresters loaded timber, so I pulled in there for a blow, got out and stood back to admire my acquisition.

Although the sight of the shining motor gave me a great feeling of well-being, it wasn't the first new form of transport I had had in my life. But I thought, despite the new car's style and beauty, that the first occasion had given me even greater pleasure.

It was the day I got my 'Black 'andled bike'.

☆   ☆   ☆

It was called a 'Swift' and it was the most beautiful thing I had ever seen.

I nearly missed it as I scuffed down the High Street in Abergranog, that cold, grey-wet Saturday afternoon.

The High Street was steep, so steep that if you didn't scuff you could easily slip on your bum if the studs on your boots were worn and, anyway, it made a lovely noise and I always did it.

But I would break my journey down the hill by stopping at the various shop windows, to look at some of my favourite things.

In the Co-op chemist's window were two large, pointed

159

bottles, one on either side of the window, standing on a shelf. They were filled with clear liquid, one red and one blue. The elegant shape and cool clarity of their contents fascinated me greatly—but more than that, they had the capacity it alter the size and build of your body.

By standing back on the edge of the pavement and working your belly in and out, the image on the bottle would appear like a distorted dwarf, and if you put your cap on back to front and stuck your tongue out, it was even better.

I could play this game for as long as Bill the Pill didn't catch sight of me. He was the boss of the chemist's shop and would come rushing out, waving his arms and shooing me away.

Next stop was Marshall's. This was a tiny sweet and tobacco shop in the front room of a terraced house, run by two sisters, one large and one small. The large one, Ginny, looked like a mountain, towering over a counter laden with jars of multicoloured sweetmeats, rock and toffee. When things got short, the bottles were filled with coloured paper, and the only luxury to be had was the brown stringy liquorice root that Bill the Pill sold.

The fact that such a plant possessed homoeopathic qualities never entered our heads, but I often wondered if the amount we ate when young had any beneficial effect on our health in later years.

Lizzy Marshall was much smaller than her sister and her head could only be seen between the jars on the counter. Sometimes, if the jars were empty of sweets and she was standing behind, it looked as if her head were actually in the jar and, with her brown-rimmed spectacles, the sight was quite weird and frightening.

Peginton's the Papers had a window full of books and games, like Ludo and Snakes and Ladders, in faded yellow boxes, dead flies and a big black cat. Trying to wake the cat by tapping on the window was another diversion which I

160

enjoyed, until Mrs Peginton would come out and stop me, telling me I was a cruel boy for trying to frighten her Sammy.

Every shop had something of interest in its window, bearing no relation to the desire of the owner to promote the wares, but giving endless entertainment to a bored little boy on a Saturday afternoon.

Powell James was the jeweller in Abergranog. He never seemed to have actual jewels in his window, and every Saturday I would check to see if there were any. There were plenty of rings, beads and brooches, but as far as I was concerned, never any real jewels.

In his other window, he had a head with a great pair of glasses on, for he also looked at eyes in the back room. He sold clocks and furniture, cutlery, saucepans, vases, paint and polish, chest expanders, torches and companion sets.

Powell James the Jewellers had on his door a green and shiny sign, that read 'OPEN'. But if you looked at it sideways, it said: 'FOR EXIDE BATTERIES'. I thought that was magic.

That particular Saturday, it was cold and dull and Bill the Pill's bottles were covered in damp, so that I couldn't see myself; Marshall's had the blinds drawn for some reason; the cat wasn't in Peginton's window; so by the time I reached the jeweller's, I had nearly lost interest.

Because it was a dark afternoon, the lights were on in the shop, so it was easy to see inside. My eye ran over the wardrobes, chests of drawers, sideboards and chairs lining the walls, the standard lamp with the big frilly shade and the mirrors reflecting each other.

I had scuffed past the jewellery window when my brain caught up with my eyes. My studded boots skidded to a halt, the jerk shooting a little stream of rain off the peak of my cap.

I didn't turn, I just walked backwards until my eyes met it again.

There, leaning against a wooden bedstead, was a bike, brand new, with a price on it.

A black 'andled bike . . . boy's size.

There were a lot of bikes in Abergranog—uprights, dropped handlebars, mostly black, some still with acetylene lamps.

There were Raleighs, BSAs, Royal Enfields, Hercules and various hybrid varieties that had spawned over the years through the genius of the amateur bike mechanics. Yan Morgan was the local wizard and could build and fit three-speeds and make dynamos that really worked.

Novelties were hard to come by in those days. An occasional milometer which ticked up the distance with varied accuracy from a screw attached to the front wheel, or a speedometer whirring away and defeating the object by adding so much resistance to the pedalling, was quite unique. Paper propellers on the handlebars, or cigarette cards tied to the fork to give a staccato effect as they flicked against the spokes, were more common. Pieces of gas-mask pipe, cut in lengths, made excellent handlebar grips and were widely sought. Gas warfare in Abergranog, thankfully, never came; if it had, it could have been very effective.

For us kids, bikes were mainly hand-me-downs, for in most families the father had the best bike and then sometimes the mother; then, if they were lucky, there might be one for the kids.

But in our family, we had no bikes. Mr Lewis next door had one, a dropped handlebar racer with red grips and leather straps on the pedals. I don't know why we had no bikes, but we didn't, and the best I could do was to cadge a ride whenever I could, on someone else's. As a result, I was not at all safe on a bike, having only had short, wobbly rides which had usually ended in disaster.

Of course, I had asked for a bike many times, and had had the promise of one 'sometime'.

'Very hard to get, bikes. With the War an' that. All the

162

metal goin' for guns an' bombs, an' tanks an' that, 'ew see,' was the usual excuse. 'If they were easier to get, 'ew could have one. We'll 'ave to see, won't we?'

Nobody would sell a bike secondhand, and when Mr Lewis next door died there was a terrible family row about who should have his racing bike, and his eldest brother left the Baptists and went over to the Congs, because of it.

There was no doubt, bikes were very valuable and cherished possessions at that time in Abergranog.

But here was a bike, boy's size. For sale.

I drew closer to the window and peered within. It shone, even though there was no chrome work, bright black. And the wheels were painted silver with aluminium paint. The crank and pedals were black and it had no three-speed, but the saddle was leather, it said on a card, and there was a little bag behind for carrying tools. And on the black handlebars was a bell, black as well. On a card were the words:

'SWIFT' MODEL UT66. 26" WHEEL. 21" FRAME.
£9 10s. PUMP EXTRA (INCLUDING PURCHASE TAX.)

My father had the 'flu and was in bed when I got home. Breathlessly, I explained to Mother about the bike.

'Just one! A "Swift", with black 'andlebars. The pump is extra. It's for sale—to anybody! The saddle is leather, it says so on a card. There's a bag for tools an' all!'

Mother listened sympathetically to my rush of anxiety. She wiped her hands on a towel and pushed back some falling strands of hair from her forehead.

'I'll go and see what your father says,' she smiled, and I felt there was more than a chance.

'Your father says to go and ask Uncle Fred to have a look at it.'

Without a word, I was off. 'Ask him to go down to Powell James's and . . .' But I was off. Out into the yard, down the alley, and off up Bowen's Pitch.

Uncle Fred was Father's eldest brother. He lived on Manor Road and worked as a mining electrician at Hafodrynys, a coal mine in the next valley.

I ran up the Pitch which was a narrow winding lane that led from the village to the top ridge of Abergranog. I was nearing the top, by the council houses, when I saw Boxy Potter and his dad coming down.

'Hiya, Lasgarn!' Boxy shouted. 'You'm lookin' puffed. Who's chasin' 'ew?'

'Nobody,' I gasped. 'I'm goin' up to my Uncle Fred's to . . .'

I just held off in time. Boxy was a sneaky sort of kid and I felt it was better to keep my mission to myself.

They walked past me, and as they did, Boxy puffed out his chest.

'We'm goin' down to James the Jeweller's. They got a bike in there, which I'm goin' to 'ave,' he said haughtily. 'It's a 'Swift', with silver wheels an' a leather saddle. P'raps I'll give 'ew a ride when I gets it.'

I kept walking, but it was automatic. As I marched on up the Pitch, hot tears filled my eyes. I would have cried out loud, but I was afraid Boxy and his dad would hear. So I just sniffed and sobbed until I got to Manor Road.

At the 'Fifteen Houses', where the Pitch joined Manor Road, I sat down on the wall opposite the Co-op stables. I felt so small and lonely, and cold. Boxy Potter was in there, first again—he always was. Why were some kids so lucky? It just wasn't fair.

It's still there today, the Co-op stables. A long brick building with a slate roof, that now houses the maintenance department of a fruit machine company. No horsey smells now; the warm, urine-stale, pungent, hay-sweet odours that wafted through the louvred windows, gone forever.

But in those days it was part of it. Situations had colour, sound and a smell in a natural form, that seemed to make things more understandable, acceptable and reassuring.

As I sat upon the wall, eyes clouded, nose running, I smelt something foreign. Sharp, acrid and frightening.

I could smell smoke.

At first I didn't even look up. I just sniffed and sniffed, as if it was all part of my misfortune. Then, as if my nose was drawn by the aroma, I looked up to the end of the building, where there was a round, shuttered vent.

Easing its way through, in gentle streams that separated in the breeze, was the cause of my distraction.

Smoke. Grey puffs of smoke.

The Co-op stables was on fire.

I sat for some time, watching it. I could see Boxy Potter's face in every cloud.

'We'm goin' down to James's', the face was saying. 'We'm goin' to buy the "Swift". P'haps 'ew can 'ave a ride. P'raps 'ew can't!'

I wasn't really old enough to know many good swears. It would have been easier if I had. 'Tits' was rude, I knew that. And it would have to do for the time.

'Tits! Tits! Tits!' I shouted. 'Tits to the bike! Tits to Boxy! Tits to James's, who don't never 'ave no jewels! And Tits to the Co-op stables!'

Why I included the Co-op stables in my venom, I'll never know, but it brought my mind back to the immediate surroundings and the smoke.

It was becoming thicker and more profuse, billowing like the funnel of a railway engine.

So, I didn't go on to my Uncle Fred's. Instead, I ran across to Tom Parry's, the Waggoner, and told him his stables was on fire.

They rescued all the horses and saved most of the building and, the following day, the Manager from the Co-op came to see Father. He said that I was a very smart lad, and they wanted to give me something for saving the horses and the property.

And that's how I got my 'Black 'andled bike'.

☆   ☆   ☆

I chuckled at the memory as I got back into my new Ford Anglia—how I treasured that bike, and how upset I was at the first blemish when I fell off and bent the mudguard.

That was the only thing about brand-new possessions, they were bound to get disfigured sooner or later, and the first mark of damage was always the one that hurt most, however minute.

It was only a matter of hours before my new car was to become defiled. Looking back, it is amusing, but at the time . . .

I arrived at Mr Jones, The Derry and parked on the road where it widened slightly, just below his gate, for his buildings lay adjacent to the highway.

His small yard was particularly muddy and the seven heifers cavorted about in it, chased by Mr Jones' collie dog who seemed to be thoroughly enjoying the chaos by splashing through the dirtiest of puddles and leaping up and down on the dung heap, without making the slightest impression on the cattle.

Eventually we got them injected and their skins measured and ear numbers recorded.

I was at the road gate, thinking I had finished, when Mr Jones announced he had two more down at Lindenchurch, about four miles away. I knew he didn't have a car of his own, so it was obvious that he was going to have to travel with me.

Fortunately there was a full, flowing brook running the ditch alongside the road, and I was relieved to see that he made a thorough job of washing his wellington boots before coming over to my new car.

'What part of Lindenchurch, is it, Mr Jones?' I asked, as I opened my door. But before he could even answer, quick as a flash, the collie dog, covered from head to tail in farm-yard mud and wet dung, dived past me and leaped onto the back seat—where he stood, tongue out and wagging his tail gleefully. The obnoxious detritus was flying everywhere, just as if it had hit an electric fan, covering windows, ceiling and the brand-new red upholstery.

'Mr Jones!' I yelled. 'Your bloody dog's in my car!'

Old Mr Jones, thumbstick in hand, smiled broadly.

'Ay, Lasgarn,' he said, jovially. ' 'E likes a ride!'

10

We were married in early March, at the Church of Saint Bartholomew. Wendel Weekes was my best man, we held our reception at the Three Ravens Club—and it rained all day.

'Happy is the bride that the sun shines on,' they say, but on our wedding day nothing could dampen our spirits; Diana looking radiant—as all brides should.

The photographs were a bit of a problem, as umbrellas had to be manipulated at all angles and the little bridesmaids covered up against the cold. But it was a wonderful day and, in typical country fashion, the 'getting away' was hair-raising, for well-wishers locked all the gates from the Three Ravens and erected barriers at every turn; but after much hilarity we eventually escaped and ten o'clock at night found us safely in our London Hotel.

The following day we flew to Juan-les-Pins in the South of France, for one week.

On the plane we travelled in company with Eric Robinson, the bandleader, his band and Pearl Carr and Teddy Johnson, who were on their way to represent Britain in the European Song Contest at Cannes, with 'Sing Little Birdie, Sing'. The presence of such celebrities gave the trip an extra boost—not that we needed any.

The very mention of the South of France conjures up in many minds a picture of the blue Mediterranean, sun-drenched beaches packed with laughing, glamorous girls and nut-brown, handsome men.

Unfortunately, in early March it was rather different. Everything seemed to be closed down, the sea was grey and the weather much the same as we had left in Ledingford — wet and windy.

Our Hotel was called the Albert, a small family concern with only one other guest, an elderly American gentleman who introduced himself on our first evening as Captain Gatewood.

Whence he acquired his captaincy we never knew, but he had been many years on the Riviera. 'Sometimes married, sometimes semi-married,' he explained, with a mischievous twinkle in his eye and a wink at Diana. A lady-killer in his day, he still possessed and knew how to use that old New England charm.

Captain Gatewood drove a white Mercedes sports car and, as we had no experience of the region, he very kindly offered to show us round, which he did with great panache.

We visited the Flower Market at Nice, had dinner at the Carlton in Cannes, played roulette at Monte Carlo and drank champagne on a yacht at St Tropez, owned by a friend of his. Indeed, he showed us everything of interest and pleasure we could possibly have wished to see. He gave us both a wonderful time and, on the day we left, he presented Diana with a bouquet of red roses.

She kissed the old gentleman on the cheek and said: 'But Captain, it's we who should have given something to you.'

'You have,' he replied, with a gentle smile. 'Both of you. You see, all the places we have visited—in fact, in most cases by the very same routes—the Hotel, the time of year—he held his hand out into the ever-present drizzle. 'Even the weather—it was the same on my honeymoon, too, with my first, my very first wife. But she was killed in a car accident three weeks later.' Diana gasped and took his hand as he continued. 'I've enjoyed watching you and reliving, maybe only a little, but some of my life when I was young.' There were tears in Diana's eyes. 'Go on,' said the old man, putting his arm gently around her shoulder and holding the other out to me. 'Go on and enjoy your happiness to the full. Remember, this life is no rehearsal—it's the real thing.'

We never saw him or heard of him again, but we often talked about him. We called our first house Gatewood and, when we moved some time later, we took the name with us.

☆ ☆ ☆

Before our first house, a modern semi-detached on the Belbury Road, we lived for some months in a flat.

It was the whole of the upper floor of a large house on the outskirts of Ledingford, owned by a genteel lady by the name of Miss Setters, who described herself as one of the *nouveau pauvre*. She was forced to 'let rooms' as she put it, due to dwindling finances, for her upbringing, whilst giving her the social graces, had not helped when it came to paying the bills.

We were her first tenants and she was quite nervous about her capabilities as a landlady.

'You will tell me if there is anything wrong,' she insisted, but we had little to complain about, apart from the vastness of our accommodation, which was not her fault.

So large were the rooms that at night, when I turned out the bedroom light at the switch by the door, Diana would have to shout: 'Over here!'—lest I should fail to find the bed.

The telephone was the other problem, for there was but one and it was situated in the spacious hallway downstairs, a league away.

Although, previously, my ears had become attuned to the ringing of a telephone at night, the new surroundings and situation altered everything. It was Diana who now heard the jangling bell first and would awaken me. Then, still half asleep, I would fumble my way to the door, across the landings, down the stairs, which were arranged in three opposing flights, and into the hall.

I always did it in the dark, for the electrics in the old house must have been installed by a bunch of drunken chimpanzees, the switches being in the most inaccessible places and the lights themselves very dim.

One night, I felt a dig in the ribs. ' 'Phone!' said Diana. Off I set upon my trek to the hallway.

Eyes half closed, I felt my way down the banisters, then along the walls, reaching out for the doors like a blind man. I arrived in the hall and made my way carefully towards the ringing 'phone on the table. As I neared it, I put out my arms towards it and enveloped Miss Setters in her long black dressing-gown.

I gasped with shock. She screamed out loud—then half collapsed upon the floor.

With one hand supporting her, I lifted the receiver and, still catching my breath, gasped, 'Hang on a minute!' as Miss Setters, arms flailing, whimpered, 'Don't hurt me! Don't hurt me!'

Diana, awakened by the commotion, came to the rescue and comforted the old lady, who had heard the 'phone long before we had and had gone to answer it.

When I picked it up again, the client, who was a farmer I knew well, was still there. 'Sorry about that,' I apologised, having regained my breath. 'These things happen in the dark.'

'Well I know it, Hugh,' he chuckled. 'I remember when I first got married me'self!'

Moving into Gatewood, on the Belbury Road, made a big difference to our way of life, for we were at last on our own and felt more complete, relaxed and extremely happy.

The blissful change in my attitude to life, however, in no way detracted my enthusiasm for veterinary practice and, if anything, enhanced it. The opportunity to come back into a warm bed when one was cold, wet and in need of comfort after a midnight calving, was absolutely marvell-

171

ous—although, it took Diana a little time to get used to it!

☆   ☆   ☆

The gas-man who used to come to the digs in Glasgow once told me: 'I enjoy my job because of the glorious uncertainty of it all!' And if that philosophy could be applied to emptying gas meters, it was certainly applicable to mixed agricultural veterinary practice, as I discovered following an unusual 'phone call, early one morning.

'Cyril Paxton here. I wondered if you could come out as soon as possible. I need your help.'

The call was indeed unusual, not in the actual request, but in the manner in which it was made. Such was the tone of the caller that I shook my head in case I was mistaken, pushed back the clothes and sat on the bedside. 'You there, Lasgarn?' The voice was firmer, yet still lacking the stormy arrogance so often associated with Paxton of Donhill. 'LASGARN! I WANT YOU HERE, IMMEDIATELY! AN EMERGENCY—COW CALVING!' or, 'GET STRAIGHT OUT HERE. MARE WITH COLIC!' was more the norm.

So to hear him say 'Cyril Paxton' and even more, to say. 'I wondered if you could come . . .' was quite unprecedented.

Ever since my earliest brush with the old tyrant, who farmed some of the best land in Herefordshire—and, one had to admit, farmed it well and with style—he had only once softened his attitude towards me. Not that I minded all that much, for I had achieved some good results at Donhill since I had started and felt that, although he would never admit it, the old man had confidence in me. Being employed by Paxton perhaps involved a certain degree of masochism, but it was quality work, with good facilities, first-class livestock and, if one accepted it as such—always a challenge.

But that summer morning, the voice at the other end of

the line had no fire or aggression. It sounded broken and pleading, almost pathetic.

'What's the matter, Mr Paxton?' I asked.

'Just come as quickly as you can,' he replied. 'I'll meet you in the yard.' And with that, he rang off.

I sat on the bed, slightly shocked at the change in the old man's attitude.

'What's the trouble?' Diana stirred from her slumbers. 'Where have you got to go?'

'Yes,' I replied, vaguely.

'Where to?' she said, sitting up and rubbing her eyes.

'Paxton's.'

'Better get a move on, Hugh,' she yawned, for even Diana knew how demanding he could be.

For some time, I sat with my back to her until she thumped me between the shoulder blades. 'Hugh! Are you all right? Answer me!'

'I'm all right, but Paxton isn't,' I said, getting up and making for the bathroom. 'Something is very wrong at Donhill—very wrong indeed.'

It was a bright, windy morning as I drove towards Easthope. Beyond the village for a couple of miles, the road was lined with great sycamores, swaying majestically like galleons on the high seas; while in the meadows the silver-headed mowing grasses shivered in confusion as the fresh breezes gusted over them.

Ten minutes and I had left the highway, rattled across the cattle grid and was speeding up the rising tarmac drive that led to Donhill. How very different from my first visit, when I had approached the formidable collection of red-bricked buildings with trepidation and no little fear, after hearing of Paxton's fiery nature and obsessive attitude. Now, I was driving purposefully, eager to get to grips with whatever problem lay ahead; but as I swung onto the yard, I could hardly believe my eyes.

173

Without exception, whenever I had met Paxton about the farm, he had been immaculately attired. Bowler-hatted, dark-suited, with a button-hole and the eternal silver-topped cane, which he would either wield like a sword or tap with staccato, machine-gun-like effect on the ground, to express his feelings.

But on that windy morning, things were very different.

The old man stood bowed and lifeless and, although he wore a suit, it hung crumpled and without shape on his unsteady frame. The cane was there, silver-topped, but static in his right hand, not a sword or machine gun, but a crutch for support. He was collarless, tieless and hatless, his white hair blown by the wind into a jumble of thin strands—and on his feet he wore carpet slippers. As I got out of the car and walked towards him I was saddened by the transformation, for here was Paxton of Donhill, a mere shadow of his former self.

'What's the matter?' I asked. 'Aren't you well?'

The wind gusted, blowing his clothes against his body as he turned half into it and shook his head.

'Sick, Lasgarn,' he replied, his features gaunt and grey. 'Sick to my heart.' He looked uncertainly at me for a moment, then, taking a deep breath, gave a flick of his cane and said: 'Follow me.'

He shuffled his slippered feet towards the house and through the side gate, into the garden. Despite the gusty start to the day, everything looked immaculate. The lawns were trim as velvet, rose bushes and shrubs strong and flourishing. As we passed through the vegetable section with its arrow-straight rows of beans and beetroot, I realised that we were making for the aviary.

We mounted the wide concrete steps and I halted, expecting him to start fiddling in his waistcoat pocket for the key. But he didn't stop.

Shuffling and grunting, he continued up the steps and pushed at the door, which surprisingly swung open with

174

just the slightest of moans from the iron hinges.

Then the old man stood back and, leaning heavily upon his cane, looked down at the floor and all but sobbed.

'Go in, Lasgarn,' he said. 'Go on in.'

It was the silence that hit me first, a cold, uncanny silence. Where previously, and especially on my first visit to Paxton's magnificent collection of exotic birds, the ear-shattering cacophony was all-embracing, now the air was hollow and empty and I felt a shiver run down my spine. Then my eye picked up the sight of the first dead bird, a little finch. It would hardly have been noticeable on the floor by my foot but for the inquisitive breeze that had sneaked in behind me, ruffling its downy breast. A simple, soft caress—otherwise, it was motionless.

As I raised my head, slowly the disaster became sickeningly obvious. Everywhere there were dead birds— bloodstained, broken, feathery carcases; some headless, others stuck in the wire meshes, strangulated in a desperate, futile attempt to escape the perpetrators of the horrendous massacre.

For that was what it was, a massacre—a vicious, wicked, senseless destruction. I stood for some time in sheer disbelief that such a terrible thing could happen, then turned to Paxton who had now come to my side, but I couldn't find words and just shook my head in dismay.

'I always come here at six in the morning. Every morning, winter and summer,' he began. 'It's my escape. When I'm not on the farm or in the office or in bed—I'm in here. *You* know what this means to me . . .' His eyes radiated a faint glimmer of his old fire as he silently reflected upon his past. And I *did* know, for that was the one and only time he had softened, until now, and had confided in me about his troubled background, not long after I had come to Ledingford.

Paxton was born up north on a large country estate. 'My father worked on the land; my mother was in service—and they were treated like dirt,' he had told me, standing practically in the same spot that we occupied now. 'I had a pet jackdaw called Barley; I gave him that name because I found him injured on the edge of a barley field. I nursed him back to health and that bird became my whole life. He would ride on my shoulder wherever we went.'

One day, while walking through the wood, Paxton met the Squire's two sons with three dogs. Barley panicked at the dogs, fluttered up into a tree and wouldn't come down. 'The boys said: "We'll get him down for you",' recalled Paxton. 'I thought they were going to get a ladder, but they came back with a gun. And they shot Barley out of the tree.'

He was only eight at the time, but that experience changed his whole personality. Until then he had been a shy, quiet boy, but he swore to get even.

When he was old enough he started buying and selling scrap. 'I worked, I sweated,' he had told me. 'I barged my way through life. By the time I was fifty I had made a fortune. Then the estate where I was born came up for sale. It was so run-down they couldn't get a bid. So what do you think they did? They came and asked me—the servant's son—if I was interested. I laughed, I laughed in their faces!'

When Paxton moved down to Herefordshire he decided to have the best land, the best crops, the best livestock and the finest collection of birds that money could buy. I remembered how he had waved his cane expansively at the vibrant, colourful scene, saying: 'And all, you might say, Lasgarn, because of a dead jackdaw.'

What an irony it was to view the scene now.

Yes. I knew what that aviary meant to him and, with the privileged knowledge of his upbringing, despite his arrogance, impatience and uncompromising manner, I liked him, even respected him. But never had I thought I would feel as I did at that moment—just downright sorry for him.

He continued to describe how he had discovered the desecration. 'But for the wind in the night, I might have heard something,' he said, 'but I just came at my normal time, opened the door and walked straight in.' Suddenly he put his hand to his forehead, as if he might faint, and I took his arm, but he shrugged it off and recovered.

'There were five of them—two ginger ones, two lean, greyish things and a black one as big as a dog.' I didn't follow, and he saw it. 'CATS, LASGARN! BLOODY CATS!' he roared in his old style; then he coughed, took a deep breath and calmed down. 'Some bastard,' he said quietly and without any venom, 'some bastard let a mob of cats loose on my birds.' Then he turned unsteadily away and, although he made little sound, his body shook and I knew he was sobbing.

I left him and walked on into the centre of the devastation. Whoever had devised such a revenge —for that was surely what it was—had an evil mind, and whatever the reason, nothing could have hit Paxton harder. Lawyers, financiers, pedigree breeders—he could match them all; but killing his birds had hit at the root of his very existence.

I cast my eye over the feathery carnage and as I did so, a soft fluttering caught my attention. Looking upwards to the rafters, I could see, perched upon the far rim of the header tank, about a dozen survivors. I picked out two cockatiels, some African grey parrots, a lovebird, some budgies and a couple of others I couldn't identify.

But below them it was awful. The finches and canaries were all dead, probably most of them from shock; but I suspected that several of the larger birds had been victims of a human hand, or a weapon wielded by one, for they appeared to have been clubbed to death.

I returned to Paxton and told him about the survivors. He scanned the roof with his watery grey eyes, but I doubted if he could readily appreciate anything.

'I want you to do what you can for those that are alive. Anything in pain or suffering I want putting out of its misery. And all the rest I want taking away—I don't want them buried at Donhill.'

I nodded in agreement, although I felt inadequate on several counts. First, I had to catch the survivors; secondly, I was not very knowledgeable on First Aid for exotics; and, lastly and most problematically, where was I going to get rid of a wagon-load of dead birds? But that wasn't all, for, as if to add to my difficulties, Paxton made one further request. 'One thing more, Lasgarn,' he said, tapping his cane on the ground in his old form. 'No one must know about this. No one. Understand?' His eyes fixed on me questioningly. I nodded, reminded of a film I had seen about the Mafia; Paxton, despite his setback, would have made the perfect 'Godfather'.

I was tempted to ask if he had any idea who it was, but he gave me no chance. 'I'll send Mason to help you. Anything you want, he'll get it. And keep the whole business to yourself.' He shuffled for the door and, as he drew it open, he turned to face me. 'You would wonder how a man could make such enemies in this Life, Lasgarn, wouldn't you?' he said, quietly. 'Or who could know what in this world I treasured most. But they're about, Lasgarn. They're about.' With that, he left, closing the door behind him.

As I turned to survey my macabre task, I sensed that even if I wasn't to know from whom the vengeance came— Paxton did. And, knowing Paxton, retribution would soon be in hand.

Mason's main care was the Hereford cattle, but he knew quite a lot about the birds, for although Paxton spent much time in the aviary, it was Mason who carried out the maintenance, cleaned the pens, saw to the more mundane requirements and took complete control when his boss was away.

He was shattered at the sight. 'The work of the Devil

himself, Mr Lasgarn,' he said, picking up a crumpled parakeet from the floor and looking at it sadly. 'Who else, in 'is right mind, would want to kill a pretty thing like this?' He pondered for a while, then, shaking his head and 'tut-tutting', opened the hessian sack he was holding and placed the dead bird gently inside.

Without Mason's help, I cannot contemplate how I would have managed, for it was he who netted the survivors, calmed them down and held them for treatment. And for a man more used to handling massive bulls such as Warrior, the Champion Stock Bull, or the wild young heifers of the herd, Mason had a surprising tenderness of touch. Once restrained, the nervous, fragile creatures lay quietly in his horny hands.

We converted the locker room, where feeding stuffs and general equipment were stored, into a temporary hospital. There were several spare show cages available and I found two electric heaters to warm the place up. There were shutters on the windows which I closed to cut out the direct sunlight and, from the house, Mason fetched some honey and water with which we syringe-fed the weaker victims, my treatment being based upon the principle that shock was the main condition to be combated.

One of the cockatiels had a broken leg which I splinted with a split pencil, applying some adhesive plaster both laterally and medially to form a sandwich to support the fractured bone. I strapped wings and patched wounds, but some of the less fortunate survivors were too savaged to repair and, as was Paxton's wish—I put them out of their pain.

It was surprising how many dead birds could be contained in one sack; even so, we filled five and a half, loading them into my car, three in the boot and the others on the back seat.

Two hours later, with my pathetic cargo aboard, I set off for the Council Incinerator.

I told only Diana the truth about my visit to Donhill and, as my colleagues assumed it had been for a calving, I did not disillusion them. So it was with some incredulity that I read a report in the *Ledingford Times* headed: 'DISASTER AT DONHILL. FANCY BIRDS SLAUGHTERED BY INTRUDERS.'

How the story got out I never knew and Paxton did not question my silence at any stage; but the whole episode caused quite a stir about the County.

On the following Monday, I had returned to St Mark's Square in time for evening surgery, when Miss Billings handed me a piece of lined notepaper, folded several times.

'A friend of yours brought it in this afternoon,' she said, smiling.

I sat down upon the bench seat and unfolded the letter. It read:

DEAR MISTER LASSGAN

GRAN TOLD ME ABOT MISTER PARTINS BIRDS AN HE LOST HIS. I GOT YUNG UNS AND BLUE AND ASSY

HE CAN HAV THEM IF I CAN KEEP BLUE.

THERE IS SOME SEEDS AN HAVE A BAG OF GRIT

YOUR FREENO

WILLIAM DENT

I couldn't stop the tears in my eyes.

'What's the matter, Mr Lasgarn?' asked Miss Billings. So I showed her the note—and she cried, too.

How this great world goes around in full circles, I thought. For it was only just over a year ago that little Billy Bent, now an orphan and living with his Gran behind the station, had come to the surgery with his blue budgie, Peter. I knew Miss Billings would remember it well. It was suffering from an impacted crop and when I attempted to reduce it surgically, the bird died under the anaesthesia.

I had told Paxton about Billy, and it was then that the old man poured out his heart to me about his own upbringing. He had replaced Peter with a pair of budgerigars, one blue and one green—and now, little Billy was offering to pay him back.

When I told Paxton about the note he smiled, a rare occasion for him. He asked me to thank Billy. 'I might take him up on the offer,' he said thoughtfully, in the same manner that he might have done had he been contemplating a deal of far greater financial importance.

With all the publicity, the police became involved and commenced investigations, and within three weeks had apprehended the culprit—an out-of-work gamekeeper of doubtful character, from a neighbouring county. But, surprisingly enough, Paxton declined to prosecute.

I taxed his reticence when next I visited Donhill, for, since the catastrophe, I had found him considerably more open and approachable.

'He was just a tool, Lasgarn,' he told me. 'Just a tool.'

'So who was really behind it?' I asked.

'Someone who has hated me from boyhood,' he replied wistfully. 'Someone who was insanely jealous of my success.'

He did not elaborate any further, but as I drove back to Ledingford, I wondered if that 'someone' was a person or persons who, many years ago, had not been content with just shooting a jackdaw called Barley out of a tree.

☆   ☆   ☆

Meanwhile I was becoming more involved in the work of the practice. I started a 'Sheep Scheme', which increased my contact with the local farming community; a project viewed by both Bob Hacker and McBean with guarded interest.

Amongst livestock, sheep, at the time, were very much second class citizens on most lowland Border farms, where cattle and pigs were of greater value and corn and hops took most of the labour. The value of a ewe was so low that it was not thought worth calling out the vet, and it was only in the event of large losses or lambing problems that we were consulted.

But science was marching ahead and the improved vaccines, more efficient worm medicines and diagnostic advances in the detection of mineral deficiencies, could not be ignored. 'Poor doing' was to a great extent accepted amongst some flocks in areas away from the rich water meadows, where rapid fattening was so predictable and effortless.

I circulated all the clients I thought would be interested, suggesting that with veterinary advice and the sensible use of the new medicines and food supplements, sheep could be made more profitable.

For thirty pounds per annum, I offered to call initially, to discuss the whole of their sheep enterprise and how it integrated with general farming policy. This meeting, I suggested, would be better held in the evening, when there were no workday distractions.

Two further 'on-farm' consultations would be given, one in the autumn and the other in the spring. Together with the advice, I was also prepared to carry out ewe *post-mortem* examinations on any that should die. For, as I pointed out, a dead sheep could be as valuable as a live one, if the cause of death could be elucidated and the knowledge used to benefit the flock in general.

The last part of the scheme involved the taking of blood samples from a representative number of the flock for mineral analysis.

I had ten farmers interested and prepared to join in with my idea. They were mostly from the north of the County, with two south of the river and one on the Black Mountain.

The acceptance from the Black Mountain pleased me greatly, for Black Mountain men were great 'sheep men' and very jealous of their local knowledge and expertise. To be fair, John Braddon was not of Black Mountain stock, being born in the North Country, where he had obtained his farming experience, before settling with his family on the rugged Border slopes.

I learned a lot about farming that summer, for my hours spent in conversation, more often than not over a meal, enriched my knowledge and awareness, not only of sheep, but of local agricultural husbandry and of something I had never expected, the characters and personalities of some most interesting and very genuine people.

The Scheme worked well, for initially there were many misunderstandings, such as the correct timing for vaccinations, or the life-cycle of sheep parasites, balanced feeding or when to give minerals. Simple corrections in strategy, but they all paid dividends.

Sometimes, at these most enjoyable meetings, the flow of information was in both directions and often beneficial in more ways than one.

At the Bennets', both Elwyn and his wife Betty joined in the discussion, for the farm business was in both their names and they took equal share in the work and responsibility.

The conversation got around to sheepdogs, and I commented on Elwyn's dog, which I had chanced to see on the way in, saying it looked fit and well up to the job.

'D'you know,' he said, 'an' the Missus won't mind me saying, but that dog saved our marriage. Didn' he, Bet?'

'Yes 'e did, Mr Lasgarn. Yes 'e did!' she exclaimed emphatically.

'Yes 'e did,' repeated Elwyn, dragging out the suspense.

'How was that?' I urged, lest after the build-up I wasn't let into the secret.

'Bin 'ere nine years,' explained Elwyn. 'Came to the place fresh married, an' it was a 'ard start. Me an' Bet would row summat terrible. Night an' day.' Betty Bennet nodded again, in enthusiastic agreement. 'Then I bought Shep, off Arty Tarrant. He was only a pup when 'e come an' I said to Arty, who was good with dogs: "Any tips on trainin' 'im?" An' Arty said, "Don' you never quarrel with your Missus in front of the dog. 'Tis bad for 'is nerves!" An' d'you know what?' said Elwyn. 'We've never rowed since!'

Arty Tarrant's advice was very sound; indeed it was a pity there was no dog about the day I went to Ivan Witts' place, to calve one of his oldest cows.

Queenie was her name, and she had produced nine single calves regularly over the years and decided to finish her career with a grand finale, by giving birth to twins. But the old lady was a trifle over-ambitious and Ivan had to ring for help when he realised that she would not manage the birth alone.

Always laughing and joking, Ivan was quite a wag and delighted in playing tricks on any unsuspecting visitor.

However, when I arrived he was in more serious vein as he came across the yard carrying a bucket of steaming water and a white towel.

I was soon stripped and about to lather up before making my preliminary examination, when I noticed there was no soap.

'Damn that!' said Ivan. 'I forgot — won't be a minute.' and

he clattered off across the yard in his heavy boots.

In fact, Ivan was all of ten minutes before he returned, and when he did, he appeared red-faced and flustered.

' 'Ad a deuce of a job to find any,' he puffed. 'The Missus is up the orchard. ' 'Ow about this?'

He held out a large oval tablet, rose pink, with a gold label at its centre.

It must have weighed at least a pound and had a perfume that would have knocked off my hat, had I been wearing one.

'Phew!' I exclaimed. 'A bit strong!'

'Your wife'll be askin' questions about where you bin,' said Ivan with a grin.

'I'll have a written statement from you before I go,' I replied, 'to prove I've only been calving a cow.'

The banter over, I washed up and set into my task.

It was quite a tangle, both calves coming, or trying to come, together, so that I was presented with an absolute confusion of heads and legs.

Once I had decided what belonged to whom, I was able to push one gently back a shade to allow its mate to ease by. When that was done, the delivery was fairly straight-forward, for the calves were not very large.

The second one had a little difficulty in breathing, and Ivan and I were busy giving it a shake by its hind legs to free its lungs of mucus, when in stormed Mrs Ada Witts.

She was a large woman and practically filled the doorway; with eyes flashing and arms akimbo, she looked quite fearsome.

'IVAN!' she screeched. 'WHERE'S MY SOAP!'

She took absolutely no notice of me, although I felt the blast of her voice; it made both Ivan and myself go quite limp, so that the little calf slid gently to the ground.

' 'AVE YOU 'AD MY SOAP!' she screeched again. This time, she took a step nearer in a rather threatening manner and, as Ivan backed away, I bent to my side and dipped into the bucket of steaming water. Fishing round, my hands sank deeply and easily into the squashy mass at the bottom of the bucket.

As I withdrew it, it oozed between my fingers, great lumps of it cascading back into the bucket.

'Is this it?' I asked, offering up the remains.

I thought Mrs Witts was going to explode, for she seemed to double in size before my very eyes, her face going purple. Like a kettle close to the boil, she simmered for a few seconds; then came the steam, in the form of a tirade of female wrath, the like of which I had never witnessed.

It transpired that the soap was very dear to her; she had won it at a raffle at the Women's Institute and was the envy of all the parish. It was highly expensive, being from a Paris salon, and she had been savouring for months the pleasure she would experience when finally she brought herself to use it. And now her prize possession was just a squidgy mess, with bits of straw and other more unsavoury elements adhering to it.

Her anger only partly defused, she eventually spun away, like a passing tornado, shouting threats and swearing reprisals all the way back to the house.

The incident took us both a little while to get over. Finally, Ivan swallowed hard. 'Dinner with the dogs for me,' he said, then glanced in my direction. 'What you laughin' for, Lasgarn? Ain't funny, yer know.'

But I couldn't control my mirth. 'I think I'm due a laugh out of you. Especially after last week.'

'Last week?' Ivan looked puzzled, then his face cleared. 'Oh, last week!'

Then he slapped his thigh and roared with laughter himself.

It had been two weeks previously that I had called at Ivan's farm to treat some young heifers with pneumonia. Ivan, in his usual jocular fashion, had been ribbing me about

186

putting on weight since I had married, and saying that Diana had been feeding me too well.

'If ever you want any spuds,' he concluded generously. 'Though you'll have to dig 'em yourself. Take as many as you like; second field off the main road, any time.'

I thanked Ivan very much and, the following Saturday afternoon, I told Diana about his offer and suggested that we drive out and get some.

I parked where the road widened and, leaving her, took my sack and garden fork into the field, where I commenced to raise some potatoes.

It was a good crop, clean and firm, and in no time at all I had quarter-filled my sack. I was about to move on to another haulm when I heard a shout:

'Oy! What do you think you're doing?'

I looked back to the road, to see a short, thick-set fellow with glasses, wearing a tweed hat, leaning on a gate.

'Digging potatoes!' I confidently replied.

'I can see that!' said the fellow in the tweed hat, rather sharply. 'An' who gave you permission?'

'Ivan Witts!' I shouted.

'So he might,' he shouted back. 'So he might. An' I'm Dan Berrington—an' that's my bloody field!'

Fortunately, Dan Berrington was a reasonable sort of chap and recognised me as Bob Hacker's assistant.

'Ivan Witts is a varmint,' he said, with a grin. 'I came up from Devon three year ago, and of all places, I had to buy a farm next to him! Take last Christmas, for instance; called on him, an' he said: "Now would you like a chicken, Dan?" I said, "That's very kind of you, Ivan," because we had no poultry at home, at the time. Bless me, when I got back to the car, there was the biggest bloody cockerel you ever did see, flyin' around inside!'

I introduced Diana to Dan, and he offered us a 'feed' of peas from an adjacent field.

'It does belong to you?' asked Diana, understandably

187

suspicious.

'Would I lead a lady astray?' replied Dan.

And believe me, from the mischievous twinkle in his eye, I wasn't too sure whether I could trust him, either.

Another commodity that was freely on offer on my travels around the County was cider. And for anyone spending more than a fleeting visit to the Borders, an acquaintance with 'Old Scrumpy' was inevitable.

It came in a variety of guises, from sharp and sweet in taste, to golden and green in colour, the appearance often more than belying its potency.

Most farmers around the County made cider in varying amounts, keeping the brew in vast, seasoned barrels. There had been a time, not too long distant, when a country labourer's wage was made up with a cider ration, and many would drink it for breakfast, dinner and tea. In fact, cider and fat bacon was all the diet they knew.

Of course, according to modern dietetic theory, rough cider causes gastric ulcers and liver damage, whilst animal fats can contribute to heart disease.

But if ever two wrongs made a right, it was cider and fat bacon.

Once the system was acclimatised, the acidity of the cider would break down any fatty particles, neutralising their ability to block up the blood vessels, and a ripe old age was achieved by all—or most of all.

This rather obvious rural combination was further proved by the fact that, to render the cider clear and sweet, a lump of uncooked fat meat was added to the fermentation and, in more unsavoury quarters, the incorporation of a rat or two was not unknown, to give it 'body'.

The cider apples would first be 'chawled' or pulped through a type of roller mill, often driven by a horse. The strong-smelling mulch, or pomace, that resulted was folded into coconut matting in wedges about six inches deep.

Several layers were stacked between the solid oak blocks of the press, which were then screwed down hard by hand, using long ash poles as levers, rather like turning the capstan of a ship.

This was known as 'Queaking the Juice' and the pure extraction was run off into a tub, before being diluted, barrelled up and allowed to ferment.

An acknowledged expert in such matters was the 'Reverend', otherwise Revington Bright, an imposing, well-educated, sometime Thespian, but latterly gentleman farmer of private means; an individual who, despite his nickname, had no connection with the cloth, and whose consuming passion for making cider was only exceeded by his passion for its consumption.

He was a tall, portly man with a red face and dark, straggling hair, a trifle wild-eyed but extremely congenial. He addressed all male acquaintances as 'my dear boy', and all females as 'madam', applying this equally to his beloved Jersey cattle and to people, for his few meadowland acres supported a small dairy herd.

My first visit to the 'Reverend' was on one of those warm, easeful days of which we had so many that summer. Yet, whilst the weather was delightful for humans, the effects were not so acceptable to the livestock, the main problem being the large hatch of flies that had emerged, especially on the river meadows. Apart from their nuisance and irritation, they spread infection, causing, among other things, acute outbreaks of mastitis amongst the cows.

One of the 'Reverend's' Jerseys had developed an extremely swollen udder resulting from such an infection, which I explained to him was of fly-borne origin and called Summer Mastitis.

After treating the problem by stripping out the udder and infusing and antibiotic mixture, I gave him some drenches to medicate his cow daily.

He thanked me for my attention and, after I had packed

189

my case and washed my hands, said: 'Now, Mr Lasgarn, how about joining me for Communion?'

Seeing that I was a trifle puzzled, he raised his fingers to his lips and waggled them, to confirm the invitation, then led off towards the house.

His cellar was situated at the rear of an old half-timbered building, cunningly concealed by large rose bushes, between which we passed to get to the door. Inside it was cool and rather gloomy, save for the shafts of sunlight that broke keenly through the splits in the stone wall.

The whole space was filled with barrels of all shapes and sizes—there must have been thirty and more, each one firmly chocked so that it wouldn't roll away.

He motioned me to sit on an old pig-killing bench; then, taking two glass tumblers from a cupboard, set them on a short plank of wood which represented a rustic tray.

He gave the tap of one of the barrels a swift turn, allowing the contents to squirt briefly into a tiny container, wired to the spout.

'To flush the flies!' he commented. Then, taking the tumblers, he filled each one just one quarter full.

'Now I want you to try this, Mr Lasgarn,' he said, proffering the glasses on the piece of plank. 'But if you don't like it, don't drink it.'

That, I felt, was being very fair, for I had heard it said that he had been responsible, on more than one occasion, for the total inebriation of his unsuspecting guests, although he himself firmly maintained that he never set out to get anyone drunk or weak-kneed. But tales were still told, like the one about the chap who came by bicycle and, after leaving, although the hill from the farm was but a few hundred yards to the main road, did three and a half miles before he got to the top, so meandering was his path.

The 'Reverend' studied my reaction as I raised the glass to my lips, and nodded with satisfaction as he saw me inhale the bouquet, even before I had tasted.

It was rich and heady, with only a hint of apple, the depth and content of the aroma suggesting much more than its appearance portrayed.

Smoothly, it rolled over my tongue and I swallowed effortlessly, giving my palate such a delectable treat that it made me close my eyes to appreciate its full flavour.

'This is superb,' I said. 'What is it?'

'Essence of the gods, my dear boy,' replied the 'Reverend', sampling his glass, 'that only a few are privileged to taste.'

The Communion went from delight to delight as we sampled on, from ciders to perry, finishing with a crystal-clear spirit that burned a hole in my tongue like an ice-cold screwdriver.

He did not elaborate on his method of manufacture, apart from saying that he used the Kingston Black apple, renowned for its potency, and matured the product in rum casks that he had sent down from an importer at Shrewsbury. He did, however, acknowledge that there were one or two personal refinements of his own, but he put his fingers to his lips at that point, to indicate that they could not be divulged.

I don't suppose that I consumed more than two full tumblers in total and, when I bade him goodbye, I felt no untoward effects, other than that the day appeared brighter and warmer, and life was very agreeable.

I drove to the main road and stopped just past the bridge, where there was a telephone box; parking the car in the adjoining lay-by, I went inside to call the surgery.

I took down the messages on my pad, thanked Miss Billings and then pushed backwards with my shoulders against the door, to get out.

It wouldn't budge.

Got it wrong, I thought—although I could have sworn that was the way I had come in.

Grinning to myself at such a stupid mistake, I heaved a

shoulder to the left, expecting to feel fresh air—but again, firm as a rock. I tried the other side—exactly the same.

I pushed high. I pushed low. I pushed right and pushed left. I couldn't find the door! I was trapped! Trapped in a GPO 'phone box!'

Now, on a summer's day, such a small enclosed kiosk can be not only claustrophobic, but also very, very hot. And the more I tried to escape, the hotter I became. I could not have sweated more, had I been in a crowded Finnish sauna.

I was all of ten minutes searching for the exit, although it seemed like an eternity, and to anyone observing the scene I must have appeared demented, for I certainly felt I was going mad.

In fact, I still don't remember the door opening, but I found myself at last, sitting on the roadside verge next to the lay-by.

It was only then, when I had cooled down, that I was able to evaluate the situation more rationally; and I decided, most definitely, that whenever I again took Communion, it would only be in church.

☆　　☆　　☆

As well as the 'Sheep Scheme', I also tried to encourage regular visits to dairy farms on a similar basis.

Milk production was on the increase in the County, which traditionally had been renowned for beef. More dairy units were resulting from the establishment of Council holdings, large farms which were split up into smaller units and rented to suitable applicants. The tenants were mostly ambitious farm workers or farmers' sons wanting to get a start in agriculture, and a small dairy herd, even on a limited number of acres, was a good way of doing it.

From the veterinary point of view, the dairy cow provided more work, and consequently income per animal, than any other livestock: mastitis, lameness, dietary problems, calving cases and infertility.

The last was most important, for although it might appear on the surface that dairy cows just produced milk for human consumption, the basic motivation for the bovine was to feed the calves. If there was no calf produced annually, there would be no milk, and so regular pregnancy was essential to the economics of the unit.

If conception did not occur between six to eight weeks after calving, another month would elapse before the cow came 'bulling' and was again receptive for fertilisation. So every lost season was a month's lost milk—which could never be reclaimed.

It was for this reason that early pregnancy diagnosis was valuable to the efficient dairy farmer.

The method in the cow, and indeed the mare, was quite exceptional, in that it was possible to palpate the womb by hand, to appreciate the viability of its contents.

It necessitated a rectal examination, which may seem distasteful to some, but was and still is the most positive and practical way of assessing the state of the womb.

An arm is passed gently inside the cow and, by opening the palm and extending the fingers whilst pressing downwards, it is possible to feel the womb beneath.

By gradually closing the hand, one can then envelop the body and both horns of the organ, albeit through the fine but sensitive barrier of the rectal wall.

In the non-pregnant state it feels like two, foot-long pieces of soft rubber pipe, joined at the posterior end to form the slightly wider body, and coiled at the free end, from which are suspended the grape-like ovaries, one on each side, like tassels adorning a gnome's cap.

Once conception occurs, the fertilised egg established within develops into an early foetus, and although the foetus itself is not appreciable, being so minute, the surrounding, fluid-filled membranes are.

By very delicately taking the wall of the womb between

the fingers and applying cautious pressure, the fine membranes can be trapped in the fingertips. Further pressure causes them to slip away because of their elastic texture, and the sensation of a 'click' is felt.

This diagnosis, of a 'foetal click', denotes early pregnancy.

To me, this experience is still one of the most fascinating and marvellous in all veterinary practice—that of actually being able physically to appreciate an unborn, but developing, new life. To be so close to creation is a profound sensation, and there are very few, other than a country vet, who ever have the privilege of knowing it.

'See with your fingers,' C.J., my old mentor, would say, when I was a student in his practice in Newpool—and in pregnancy diagnosis that 'sight' is unique.

As the foetus develops, diagnosis becomes easier as the womb enlarges and, at about sixteen weeks, the cotyledons or 'buttons'—raised areas where the calf's membranes are attached to receive nutriment—can be felt. Later, the calf itself is evident, but although its presence is that much more obvious, the wonder still remains.

A positive diagnosis, however, is no guarantee that the calf will be carried to full term. Occasionally, in the early stages, the foetus can be re-absorbed, or in the later stages, aborted. The causes are many and varied, so that conception and live birth are never a foregone conclusion, nature dictating the degree of success all the way.

To true country folk, and to those who live close to the soil, such caprices of procreation are often more readily accepted than by others brought up in differing circumstances, where black is black and white very much white.

There was Colonel Blaghorn, Queen's Hussars, Rtd., a huntin' shootin' and fishin' gentleman who asked me to examine a bunch of Friesian heifers that he had 'running with the bull'.

When I arrived at his farmstead, the military influence

was all too obvious, for, like the Phippsons', everything was orderly and upright.

Even the heifers were lined up, each with a spotless rope halter and, standing by, practically to attention, was the cowman.

'I'll tell the Colonel you're here, sir,' he rapped out in a Sergeant Major's bark, departing at the double to the big house.

The Colonel, duly summoned, came to oversee the proceedings. He was exceptionally tall and erect, with a flowing ginger moustache, pointed features and a very direct manner.

I commenced my rectal examination on the first of the six heifers. Carefully, I investigated the pelvic area, the heifer standing quietly and patiently, while I collected the horns and the body of her womb into my grasp and gingerly compressed the walls to elicit the 'foetal click'. But the horns were compact and solid, there was no fluid or foetal content; she was non-pregnant.

I announced my negative findings, which were received in silence.

On to the next one—again, non-pregnant. And the next. And the next.

At the fifth negative result, the Colonel could contain himself no longer.

'But, Mr Lasgarn!' he spluttered furiously. 'They must be, man! They must be!'

His comment was in the nature of a command, but it was one that even the Colonel, with all his military precision and control, could not enforce.

I came to the sixth and last. Again, the spreading of the palm, the closing of the fingers, the gentle pressure, the slight squeeze and, 'CLICK'—the sixth was in calf.

Turning to the Colonel, I announced the good news.

He pushed back his shoulders, smiled, brushed his moustache with the bent knuckle of his left hand, then took a step forward and laid a hand upon my shoulder. Looking at me as if I had been personally instrumental in achieving the conception and had done it solely for Queen and Country, he said in a firm, emotional tone:

'Well done, Mr Lasgarn. Well done!'

I told Diana about the experience and she, too, appreciated the humour of the situation.

It was some weeks later that I met her for lunch in Ledingford.

As she came towards me across High Town, her eyes were sparkling and her face alight with happiness. She had just come from a visit to Dr Brown.

I didn't have to ask, for when she reached me, she kissed me on the cheek and whispered: 'Well done, Mr Lasgarn. Well done!'

11

The prospect of becoming a 'family man' made me suddenly realise that life was running on at quite a pace. Whilst, in some respects, it demanded an extra responsibility on my part, it was a most satisfying state—one of maturity.

Yet it was still coupled in my mind with a bewildering excitement for the future.

That autumn, Diana and I felt very much together. We spent a lot of time in the countryside, for that, too, was in a state of satisfaction and tranquillity following the good harvest.

We wandered by the river, in the woods and sometimes on the Black Mountain—and at nights we painted and decorated the small bedroom, ready for the new arrival.

Life was so full that Christmas rather took us by surprise, but soon the bonhomie of the season was upon us, and Herefordshire was alive with poultry, holly, good cheer and all thing festive.

I was leaving for the surgery one morning, just as the postman arrived.

'Twenty cards, three parcels and no bills,' announced Terry, handing over the bundle cheerfully. 'And Old Duffy would like you to call. His Christmas goose is ill.'

Now, Old Duffy was an Irish tinker living in a tumble-down caravan, with his skewbald pony and three dogs, on the edge of Gurney's hop yard.

Gurney's was out on the Belbury Road about three miles past my place, and if ever Duffy wanted anything, he sent a message via the postman, but in a verbal form.

I thanked Terry for the information and resolved to call on the old chap that afternoon.

Just after two o'clock, I parked my car at the hop yard gate and set off with my medical bag along the path that skirted the naked poles and wires. Soon the smell of woodsmoke was in my nostrils and, as I rounded the far hedgerow, Duffy's dogs came racing up to greet me.

'Lie back now, me boyos,' he shouted. 'An' let the veterinary be.'

Next thing, I was inside Duffy's poky, smoky abode drinking tea from a tin mug.

'Good of ye to call now, Mr Lasgarn,' he commenced. 'Never bought a goose at this time, before. Cost me a fair penny, so she did. Brought her straight home an' fed her well. Then, t'was last night, she sat down an' hasn't so much as moved a feather since.'

I sat, supping my tea and studying the subject of Duffy's concern as she lay, quite contentedly, in an old orange box full of straw, on the caravan floor.

'How long have you had her?' I enquired.

'Bought her last Wednesday at Ledingford Market,' said Duffy. 'Liked the look of her straight away.'

He passed the big grey bird to me and she settled down happily on my lap. Running my hands over her well-covered frame, I gave her a general examination. It wasn't difficult to find the trouble.

'Overfeeding, Duffy,' I announced. 'Her crop is full to bursting.'

He leaned across and took the bird back into his arms.

'Well, I had a bit of corn saved,' he said, giving me a mischievous wink. 'She tucked into it fine an' all. But now, what can we do?'

'A little liquid paraffin should do the trick,' I replied. 'And it won't affect the taste in any way.'

'The taste?' he queried, as the goose tucked her head

under his arm. 'Now, I didn't know that a goose could taste, so I didn't!'

Suddenly a feeling of guilt crept over me, which Duffy sensed immediately.

'Now, ye wouldn't be thinkin' what I think yer thinkin',' he said, with a wry look upon his weathered face.

'Of course not,' I said, fingers crossed behind my back.

The old tinker stroked the fine down on his goose's neck.

'To be sure an' I wouldn't be eatin' Matilda for Christmas — she's me pet.'

And if ever I saw a goose smile — that was the day.

☆ ☆ ☆

Christmas passed, and the first snow came early in January. It was unexpected and heavy, blanketing the countryside. Smoothly and evenly it began — then the east wind took a hand and, with a chilling but artistic sense of delight, blew the snow from the fields into the by-ways, stifling all movement; the iced-cake drifts, obliterating hedgerows and gateways into uniquely sculptured friezes, whose virginal beauty belied the problems they caused.

But the sun shone, pressure was high and it was a fascinating time to be about — if you could get about. Often progress by car was arrested within a mile or so of the farm, where one had to be met by tractor and continue the journey in a cold and windswept fashion to the patient.

A great deal of telephoned advice was given at that time, and I had particularly long conversations with John Braddon, the Black Mountain member of my Sheep Scheme, who was completely isolated in the Shepwall Valley.

John, who was an intelligent and progressive type of man, had decided to upgrade his flock by crossing some of his better Welsh Mountain ewes with a Border Leicester ram to produce a Welsh Half-Bred.

The indigenous hill sheep were small and hardy, having the speed of light and Houdini-like qualities when confined. They could leap gates or hurdles six feet high, or burrow like moles through the thickest cover. The Half-Breds were more docile and manageable by comparison and would hopefully produce a better quality lamb. They would, however, lack the hardiness and resilience of the Welsh to combat the adverse weather of the Mountain, and it was John's intention to bring them off the slopes and house them a few weeks before lambing rather than leave them out, as was normal practice.

I had been over to his farm several times during the autumn, and we had thoroughly discussed every aspect of the idea. I covered every detail of the project with him in depth to ensure its success, for it was on my recommendation that he was doing it at all and I felt a particular responsibility towards the enterprise.

He had constructed a new building for the purpose and we had deliberated for hours over the ventilation, the drainage, trough space and lighting, so that conditions would be as near perfect as possible to accommodate the fifty Half-Breds.

By a stroke of good fortune, John had anticipated the change in the weather and had brought them in the night before the snow fell. It meant that they would be housed for a longer period than we had anticipated, for they were not due to lamb until early March. Four weeks' housing would have been quite adequate under normal conditions, but now they could well be in for two months' confinement.

We talked about feeding, for the advancing of the arrangements would put a greater strain upon the food resources. It was decided to feed hay up to early February, then introduce a concentrate ration of half oats and barley, with added minerals.

I had explained to John how the lambs double their birth-weight during the last six weeks of pregnancy, hence the feed intake would need to be gradually increased to provide adequate nutrition for both mother and the developing young.

It was the third week in February when I heard from him; there was trouble with the Half-Breds and he wanted me to go out.

'Several have become very lethargic,' he told me over the 'phone. 'They are reluctant to eat, and just lie staring into space, as if they are in a trance.' He sounded very perturbed about them; thankfully, however, although the snow had persisted, the roads were by then clear, and I was able to get to his place.

'Look at those, up there,' said John, pointing to the pure Welsh ewes tucking into some loose hay around the buildings. 'Fit as fleas, on next to nothing. Yet the Half-Breds, who are getting special attention, are going off their legs.'

Inside the shed, it was warm but not stuffy—the ventilation was adequate, anyway.

The troughs still contained feed and, when I scooped up a handful, it smelt sweet and was not dusty. But the flock around were unnaturally quiet and not the least perturbed at the entry of a stranger, as most sheep would be.

'I know they're used to me coming in and out,' remarked John, 'but look at their reaction to you. Absolutely nil. Surely, Hugh, they should be livelier than this?'

There were six ewes penned from the rest—all recumbent. Four just sat staring into space and chewing aimlessly, another seemed to be having a mild fit and was twitching and jerking spasmodically, while the sixth looked very sick indeed and was lying on her side.

I spent a considerable time examining them. They were all in good condition—very good, in fact. Their backs were flat and well covered, not a bone to be felt—but they couldn't stand, they didn't respond to noise and were blind.

201

The Half-Breds were suffering from Pregnancy Toxaemia.

John Braddon, in quite an unconnected way, put it differently:

'Perhaps I'm killing them with kindness!' he remarked.

'That's just it,' I agreed and, leaning on the pen rails, I explained the cause of the trouble to him.

'Because you had to bring them in earlier than we had anticipated, they got extra feed and the ewes put on more fat than they would have otherwise.' John nodded. 'Then,' I continued, 'during the last two weeks you've been increasing the ration.'

'You agreed that was right,' cut in John.

'Yes I did,' I admitted, 'but I was wrong! You see, that increased the unborn lamb size rapidly, the extra weight slowing the ewes down, as they were already overfat, and reducing the room inside them for food intake.'

'They have been leaving their grub,' agreed John. 'But why the blindness?'

'Well,' I explained, 'just because the ewes aren't eating, doesn't reduce the growth of the lambs, and as most of your ewes will be carrying twins, the demand is considerable. In order to supply them with nutriment, the ewe digests her own body fat—and that's when the trouble starts.'

'How?' said John, looking decidedly depressed. I continued to explain, probably for my own good as much as his, for I was personally attempting to convince myself that my conclusions were correct.

'The broken-down fats produce toxic by-products called "ketones". "Ketosis" is, in fact, another name for the condition and it's these "ketones" that damage nerve cells, as well as kidney and liver tissue.

'Oh, God!' said John. 'So they'll die!'

I had to admit, the prognosis was pretty grim.

'I'll inject glucose and dose them with glycerol, which will convert into available sugar. And I'll give some calcium and magnesium where it's needed, but once the cells are damaged it's impossible to reverse the situation. You see, even though there's plenty of food and they'd like to eat, they can't. They just haven't got the capacity—it's a straightforward lack of space.'

'How about bringing the lambs on to reduce the demand?' asked John.

'Induction,' I said. 'Too dangerous. I'd have to use drugs, and the only ones I've got are very unpredictable. Perhaps one day they'll discover something better, but at the moment that treatment could result in dead lambs and a dead ewe. On the other hand, if the lambs abort naturally, even though they are premature and might die—at the least the ewes would live. And that's the best we can hope for.'

I hated saying that, but it was true. Of course, I couldn't have known about the weather and the need for the early housing, but I did feel responsible for the problem, having encouraged John to join my Scheme.

I drenched and injected and decided the rest should be let out in the yards, even if there was a risk of pneumonia, in the hope that the exercise might encourage appetite.

If they would only lamb, the trouble would be over, but the starting date was two weeks away at least.

Over the next ten days, despite my constant attention and medication, John Braddon lost fifteen of the Half-Breds and had several abortions and premature lambs.

I was finding life tough, not only because of that particular problem, but because the practice was very busy, with emergency calls nearly every night, and calving cases and lambings constantly throughout the days.

Diana was beginning to feel very tired, and my comings and goings during the night did not help.

On the advice of Dr Brown, she rested as much as she could, but despite this, her ankles started to swell and, on the Tuesday morning, I called him for advice. He listened to my description of her symptoms and said he would come by during the afternoon.

I got back to surgery about two o'clock, having finished the morning run at Braddon's. He was still losing ewes and I was sick to death of the problem—having no answer.

'Your wife,' said Miss Billings. 'The doctor is calling again at three o'clock and he'd like you to be there.'

Diana was feeling weak and running a temperature when I arrived home. She seemed far worse than when I had left in the morning, and although she insisted she was 'not so bad', her condition worried me.

Just after three, Doctor Brown arrived. A tall, softly spoken Scot, he followed me up the stairs to the bedroom, where he gave Diana another thorough examination. He concluded by taking her blood pressure—up until then, he had made very little comment.

I stood about uneasily while he carefully and deliberately folded away his equipment. Then he sat on the edge of the bed and clasped his hands.

'What's the verdict?' I asked, attempting a cheerful tone.

He looked across at me. 'I'd like Diana to come into hospital,' he said quietly.

'Hospital!' I was alarmed. 'Already?'

He nodded.

'But why . . . what . . .?' I asked.

'Her pressure's up a bit, and in hospital we can keep a closer watch on things. With the baby due in a couple of weeks, it's the best thing.'

I didn't question him any further. 'I'll make all the arrangements and call you. Probably this evening,' he concluded.

He obviously expected a further discussion, for instead of making for the porch when he got downstairs, he turned into the lounge.

He stood by as I entered, waving me through. Then he shut the door, just as if it were his own home.

'It's 140 over 90,' he said. 'Too high for safety.'

'But Diana's blood pressure was normal at the last check,' I said. 'Why the sudden rise?'

His reply, though given in his soft, Scottish voice, shocked me to the core:

'Pregnancy Toxaemia,' he said. 'Are you familiar with it?'

I sat down and, cold and shattered, listened to his clinical explanation of the hypertension and oedema. If proteinuria developed, kidney damage could not be ruled out, and he told me that Diana needed complete rest with constant monitoring of her pressure.

My throat was full and I found it difficult to talk or ask any questions.

The predisposing factors in humans were uncertain, Doctor Brown continued, and swelling of the ankles was often the first sign.

'What about Ketosis?' I finally managed to ask.

'Ketosis!' He looked at me with puzzled surprise. 'Hugh, if ever it gets to that stage, we are in very serious trouble!' He shook his head, as if he couldn't believe the question, then he said, 'Why on earth should you ask that?'

So I told Doctor Brown all about the trouble at John Braddon's—how I was beaten as to a cure and why, with the deaths and my dilemma over induction, I felt so much anguish.

He listened attentively and when I had concluded, he nodded, as if he understood my feelings.

'Rest assured, Hugh,' he said. 'Diana's case is very different.'

'But Pregnancy Toxaemia!' I repeated.

'It is possible that due to the differing metabolic requirements of animals, particularly ruminants, the susceptibility and intensity differs. You understand ovine digestion better than I do, but I should think that having five stomachs and twins aboard is much more of a problem. Don't worry, Hugh.' He stood up to go. 'Diana's not in any way as bad as that. I'll ring you as soon as I've arranged a bed.'

He shook my hand and left.

Diana went into the County Hospital that night.

When I came home, I didn't go to bed. I sat in a chair and put a record on our small player: Saint-Saëns' Third Violin Concerto. How that brings back memories!

The piece has such depth of vigour and expression, clear, thrilling heights plunging into massive troughs— powerful, emotional. How it fitted my mood. That night, Saint-Saëns pulled me through—for, God, I was depressed.

For ten days, although I visited Diana regularly and everyone was helpful and sympathetic, particularly Brad, who cooked my evening meal—life lost all it's colour. It was cold, grey and empty. Work became a drudgery and, despite Doctor Brown's confident assurance that Diana's case was different, I couldn't get Braddon's sheep out of my mind.

Prince Andrew had recently been born and the placards were full of it . . . 'The Nation Rejoices'. 'A Fine Son for Her Majesty'. But I didn't feel like waving any flags as I drove to the County Hospital.

Doctor Brown met me in the corridor.

'I think we are going to have to hurry things along,' he told me.

'Induction?'

'That or a caesarian,' he said. 'I don't know yet.'

'Does Diana know?' I asked.

'I haven't told her—it might be a good idea if we broached the subject while you're here.'

They had moved Diana's bed near the door—where I got the idea from, I don't know, but someone once told me that was a bad sign.

She looked pale and rather sad, but she smiled and held my hand.

'A caesarian,' she said, when Doctor Brown finished his

short chat. 'Hope you have enough help . . .!'

Doctor Brown looked puzzled.

I told him about the time at Wormcastle, and how Diana had been my assistant.

'Well, then, you've got nothing to worry about, have you?' he said.

She smiled at me, but I could see in her eyes she was thinking of poor old Plum Five. Then she squeezed my hand tightly.

'Of course I haven't,' she replied.

I smiled too, but weakly. It was all I could do.

The next twenty-four hours were critical. By the following morning, no decision had been made. When I visited at night, there was still no progress.

But, when I rang at six o'clock the following morning, the Night Sister told me induction had been carried out, and a caesarian was most unlikely. That, I thought, was a blessing in itself. 'Ring again about ten,' she said brightly, then she was gone.

Later, I called the surgery, spoke to Miss Billings and told her I wouldn't be in. Bob Hacker and McBean were prepared for that and Miss Billings asked me to give Diana her love and hoped everything would go well.

'Oh, by the way,' she added, 'Mr Braddon rang. He's had three sets of twins in the night, all perfectly healthy, and the main part of the flock are starting and things should be all right now. He said, he thought you'd like to know!'

I couldn't sit about, so I got into the car and drove out to Bredstone Hill.

It was a bright, clear March morning. There had been a slight frost early on that sharpened the air and gave a keen edge to every hill and woodland. At the top, I pulled in and looked down towards the river, its lazy flow hardly perceptible as it mirrored the early sunshine, the fields beyond already ploughed in rich, dark furrows.

The cattle had been turned out in many places. Deep red

Herefords with calves afoot, and sheep—the early lowland lambers—thick upon the grass.

Spring about me, but winter in my heart.

I looked at my watch—nine-thirty.

'Ten o'clock', she had said, but I could wait no longer.

I knew exactly what I would do and where I would telephone from: the box near Granstone, the one that I got shut inside after my 'Communion' with Revington Bright.

It took ages to get connected, and as I waited, through the glass panels I looked across the countryside.

In the distance, sharp and clear in the morning sun—fifteen miles away and yet so close—the Black Mountain.

I kept my eyes upon it all the time.

And then the Sister said: 'It's a little girl—and your wife is fine . . .'

I just said: 'Thank you.'

'You can call any time,' she said.

And again I just said, 'Thank you.'

But when I got out of that box—and I did it first time . . . I threw my cap into the air and let out the loudest 'YIPPEEE!' that even fifteen miles away, John Braddon, his Half-Breds and that old Black Mountain must surely have heard—and raised a cheer too!

My winter had suddenly turned to spring—and all was joy and colour and happiness once more.